Library of
Davidson College

Quotations from Henry James

Selected by Louis Auchincloss

Quotations from Henry James

Selected by Louis Auchincloss

Published for the Associates of the University of Virginia Library by the University Press of Virginia, Charlottesville

THE UNIVERSITY PRESS OF VIRGINIA
Copyright © 1984 by the Rector and Visitors
of the University of Virginia
First published 1984

Library of Congress Cataloging in Publication Data
James, Henry, 1843–1916.
  Quotations from Henry James.
  1. James, Henry, 1843–1916—Quotations. I. Auchincloss
Louis. II. Title.
PS2112.A93 1984   813'.4   84-10428
ISBN 0-8139-1037-4
Frontispiece Courtesy of the Smith College Archives

Printed in the United States of America

For Waller Barrett
Collector and student of Henry James,
who encouraged me to complete
this collection

Contents

Introduction	ix
Characters	1
Things	17
Dialogues	25
English Hours	35
Paintings	49
Faces and Figures	55
The American Scene	71
Personalities	85
Portraits of Places	97
Scenes of Tension	109
Writers and Other Artists	121
New York	129
Literary Criticism	137
The Art of The Novel	147
Here and There	153
Sentences and Phrases	161

Introduction

To mark the two extremes of fiction one might play the game of inventing two classes, putting at one end authors who wrote primarily to "get on" with their stories and get them told, such as Dreiser, Trollope, Zola, and even Tolstoi, and at the other, those who wrote for the pleasure of telling their stories, the "mandarins," to use Cyril Connolly's term: Meredith, Flaubert, Walter Pater, Proust, and, of course, Henry James. With James, as with any great artist, the hope and aspiration had to be that the whole would prove greater than its parts, but those parts were nonetheless so lovingly and cunningly molded that, should the completed work ever fall apart, each fragment could have a proud existence of its own, like a figure from the capital of a Romanesque column. Of his last, unfinished novel, *The Ivory Tower*, each chapter and scene is as exquisite as any that he ever wrote, although one suspects that his overall scheme may have been too subtle and fanciful to have succeeded. It was in considering the satisfaction given me by those mere shards of his final work that I decided to compile the selections in this volume.

Because so many of James's landscapes and cityscapes, his houses and interiors, are brilliantly delineated and because the physiognomy of his characters is always so vividly depicted, it is often said that he had a "painter's eye." The term merits some discussion in any collection of his "word pictures." Does it mean that James could have been a painter? Probably not, as his friend and art instructor, John La Farge, saw at an early date, wisely advising his pupil to stick to letters and consoling him with the axiom that all the arts are basically one. Had James become a painter, he would probably have done portraits and landscapes in the manner of Sargent—or at least as close to that manner as he was able. He wrote exuberantly of Sargent that with him perception was by itself "a kind of execution," that the process by which the object seen resolved itself into the object pictured was so immediate as to make painting "pure tact of vision, a simple manner of feeling." James's enthusiasm for his younger compatriot was perhaps as close as he came to accepting the impressionist movement.

Some critics have been so distressed at James's failure to appreciate the impressionist school that they have sought to explain it away. John L. Sweeney, in his anthology of James's art criticisms, tries to find evidence in a single reference to "wondrous examples" of Manet, Degas, and Monet in an American collection to prove that James was finally (in 1905) converted to the movement. But there seems to be nothing else in his pieces on art to persuade us that he had any eye but for representational, academic painting. He liked Watts, Leighton, Burne-Jones, Bastien Lepage, Alma Tadema. An undistinguished taste in painting, of course, has nothing to do with the quality of a writer's work. What I am seeking to bring out here is that James liked pictures that seemed to him to depict the world as *he* saw it. But what *he* saw, he reproduced with his own art, the art of language, and it then came out, not merely as polished as a saber in a Meissonier battlefield or as tawny as a martyr-devouring lion in a Gérôme arena; it was also as shimmering as a Monet lily pond and as bright as a Renoir sky. James became an impressionist, one might almost say, in spite of himself.

When his peculiar sense of the beauty of the world around him happened to fuse with the central purpose of the novel that he was writing, he achieved his finest results. The theme of *The Ambassadors* is the cataclysmic effect of the vision of Paris on a middle-aged, middle-class American widower whose sensitivities have been starved but not destroyed by the cultural aridity of a New England small town. We see the whole book through Strether's consciousness, and the prose that evokes the glory of the French capital makes us share with the protagonist his sense of the obliteration of the moral claims of Mrs. Newsome and the town of Woolett, Mass. He "sees" them at last, as mere children, who play at living, and we see them too, as he sees them. In *The Wings of the Dove* James's theme is the plight of a young woman who is given the capacity to enjoy all the finest things in life and the means to encompass them, only to discover that she is dying. Here the prose that shows her encased in the "great gilded shell" of her Venetian palazzo, immured, so to speak, in her own lacquered coffin, intensifies our sense of the pathos of her fate by establishing the full emotional value of what she must forego.

I have found in a lifetime of reading James that my appreciation of parts of his books is at times almost as great as my appreciation of the whole. I feel that the very essence of the master can be conveyed in fragments; that I can open *The American Scene*, for example, a work of nonfiction, at almost any place, with as much pleasure as *The Golden Bowl* or *The Wings of the Dove*. Obviously, I do not belong to the school that finds James's early style crystal clear in contrast to the opaqueness of the later, the so-called old pretender's, and deplores James's elaborate revision of his novels and tales for the Scribner edition of 1907–9. I affirm, on the contrary, that his entire life was dedicated to the embellishment of a style that he continued to improve until the end.

A goodly percentage of the selections in this volume are pictures of persons and places. Fiction to James was always the story of a particular person in a particular place. His characters are apt to be closely associated with their lodgings; one pictures Gilbert Osmond lazily contemplating his evil schemes, high on a hill over Florence in a mouldering, picturesque villa; and Mrs. Lowder encased in her gleaming porcelains and shining satins at Lancaster Gate; and Adam Verver knocking the balls around in the billiard room at Fawns. And where else could one see Mrs. Gereth but presiding over the spoils of Poynton? Or Maria Gostrey but cozily settled in her precious little *boîte* of a flat in the Quartier Marboeuf? Edmund Wilson called Edith Wharton the pioneer and poet of interior decoration, but the poet is almost too specific. Her picture of the interior of the Archer's New York brownstone in *The Age of Innocence* is like a brilliant-colored photograph; we are permitted no alternatives. Imaginative readers, on the other hand, would vary widely in the way they might reproduce Madame de Vionnet's *hôtel* in the Rue de Bellechasse; all, however, would agree that it was a beautiful harmony of personal taste with inherited things.

Samples of James's dialogues make one wonder why he failed as a playwright. Of course, in the late novels and tales the diction had become too elaborately chiseled for stage use, but that is not so of his early and middle periods, where whole verbal interchanges could be lifted bodily out of the text and effectively dramatized. I believe that James might have become a more successful dramatist had he started earlier and in a humbler frame of mind. Unhappily, he waited until middle age before turning his full energies to the stage, with the wholly unjustified conviction that he had "the French theatre in his pocket." Why the emulator of Augier, Pailleron, and Dumas *fils* should have so self-confidently produced four anaemic, chattering parlor comedies that read like parodies of Oscar Wilde must remain one of the mysteries of literature.

Dramatic interest, of course, is a quality as necessary to fiction as it is to the stage, and no novelist has more deeply saturated his prose with it than James. *The Turn of the Screw* is so fine an example of sustained, unified tenseness of atmosphere that I found it difficult to isolate a sample that would stand by itself. That is true as well of the wonderful scene in *The Golden Bowl* between Maggie and the Prince in a carriage returning home from a dinner party where, without a word of dialogue or a twitch of action, a silent struggle is enacted in which Maggie resists being drawn into the surrender of her moral identity to her husband's radiated sexual attraction.

Well, why pick and choose at all? There is James, his riches overflowing the shelf and available to all. True, but there are always those who quail before such a mass. The purpose of this compilation is twofold: first, that it may bring to those having only a limited acquaintance with the master a sense of his range and variety that may induce them to read further, and second, to provide devotees of his art with a handy reader in which to revisit choice bits.

The quotations have been culled from the entire oeuvre of James and from his letters, collected and edited by Percy Lubbock and later by Leon Edel. In most cases, where I could, I have used the text of the New York edition of the novels and tales, Charles Scribner's Sons, 1907–9.

I have, in a very few instances and without using ellipses, eliminated from the body of a quotation sentences not strictly relevant to the material quoted. The collection is not so much for scholars as for those who may find pleasure in a guided browsing in the Master's prose.

Louis Auchincloss

Characters

Mrs. Farrinder

Mrs. Farrinder imposed herself. There was a lithographic smoothness about her, and a mixture of the American matron and the public character. There was something public in her eye, which was large, cold, and quiet; it had acquired a sort of exposed reticence from the habit of looking down from a lecture-desk, over a sea of heads, while its distinguished owner was eulogised by a leading citizen. Mrs. Farrinder, at almost any time, had the air of being introduced by a few remarks. She talked with great slowness and distinctness, and evidently a high sense of responsibility; she pronounced every syllable of every word and insisted on being explicit. If, in conversation with her, you attempted to take anything for granted, or to jump two or three steps at a time, she paused, looking at you with a cold patience, as if she knew that trick, and then went on at her own measured pace. She lectured on temperance and the rights of women; the ends she laboured for were to give the ballot to every woman in the country and to take the flowing bowl from every man.

THE BOSTONIANS, Chapter 4

Madame de Brécourt

She was the largest, heaviest member of the family, and in the Vendée was thought majestic despite the old clothes she fondly affected and which added to her look of having come down from a remote past or reverted to it. She was at bottom an excellent woman, but she wrote *Roy* and *foy* like her husband, and the action of her mind was wholly restricted to questions of relationship and alliance. She had extraordinary patience of research and tenacity of grasp for a clue, and viewed people solely in the light projected upon them by others; that is, not as good or wicked, ugly or handsome, wise or foolish, but as grandsons, nephews, uncles and aunts, brothers and sisters-in-law, cousins and second cousins. You might have supposed, to listen to her, that human beings were susceptible of no attribute but that of a dwindling or thickening consanguinity.

THE REVERBERATOR, Chapter 7

Mr. and Mrs. Monarch

Their good looks had been their capital, and they had good-humouredly made the most of the career that this resource marked out for them. It was in their faces, the blankness, the deep intellectual repose of the twenty years of country-house visiting that had given them pleasant intonations. I could see the sunny drawing-rooms, sprinkled with periodicals she didn't read, in which Mrs. Monarch had continuously sat; I could see the wet shrubberies in which she had walked, equipped to admiration for either exercise. I could see the rich covers the Major had helped to shoot and the wonderful garments in which, late at night, he repaired to the smoking-room to talk about them. I could imagine their leggings and waterproofs, their knowing tweeds and rugs, their rolls of sticks and cases of tackle and neat umbrellas; and I could evoke the exact appearance of their servants and the compact variety of their luggage on platforms of country stations.

THE REAL THING

Mrs. Rooth

Mrs. Rooth found no play too tedious, no entr'acte too long, no *baignoire* too hot, no tissue of incidents too complicated, no situation too unnatural and no sentiments too sublime. She gave Sherringham the measure of her power to sit and sit—an accomplishment to which she owed, in the struggle for existence, such superiority as she might be said to have achieved. She could outsit everyone, everything else; looking as if she had acquired the practice in repeated years of small frugality combined with large leisure—periods when she had nothing but time to spend and had learned to calculate, in any situation, how long she could stay. "Staying" was so often a saving—a saving of candles, of fire and even (for it sometimes implied a vision of light refreshment) of food. Sherringham made indeed without difficulty the reflection that her life might have taught her the reality of things, at the same time that he could scarcely help thinking it clever of her to have so persistently declined the lesson.

THE TRAGIC MUSE, Chapter 12

Lord Theign

Obviously, at this rate, he had passion for simplicity—simplicity, above all, of relation with you, and would show you, with the last subtlety of displeasure, his impatience of your attempting anything more with himself. With such an ideal of decent ease he would confound you, "sink" a hundred other attributes—or the recognition at least and the formulation of them—that you might abjectly have taken for granted in him: just to show you that in a beastly vulgar age you had, and small wonder, a beastly vulgar imagination. He sank thus, surely, in defiance of insistent vulgarity, half his consciousness of his advantages, flattering himself that mere facility and amiability, a true effective, a positively ideal suppression of reference in any one to anything that might complicate, alone floated above.

THE OUTCRY, Book 1, Chapter 6

Miriam Rooth

It came over him suddenly that so far from there being any question of her having the histrionic nature, she simply had it in such perfection that she was always acting; that her existence was a series of parts assumed for the moment, each changed for the next, before the perpetual mirror of some curiosity or admiration or wonder—some spectatorship that she perceived or imagined in the people about her. It struck him abruptly that a woman whose only being was to "make believe," to make believe that she had any and every being that you liked, that would serve a purpose, produce a certain effect, and whose identity resided in the continuity of her personations, so that she had no moral privacy, as he phrased it to himself, but lived in a high wind of exhibition, of figuration—such a woman was a kind of monster, in whom of necessity there would be nothing to like, because there would be nothing to take hold of.

THE TRAGIC MUSE, Chapter 10

Lord Northmore

His lordship had been a person, in fact, in connection with whom there was almost nothing but the fine monotony of his success to mention. This success had been his profession, his means as well as his end; so that his career admitted of no other description and demanded, indeed suffered, no further analysis. He had made politics, he had made literature, he had made land, he had made a bad manner and a great many mistakes, he had made a gallant, foolish wife, two extravagant sons, and four awkward daughters—he had made everything, as he could have made almost anything, thoroughly pay.

THE ABASEMENT OF THE NORTHMORES

Miss Mumby

Miss Mumby had been to Europe, and he saw soon enough how there was nowhere one could say she hadn't gone and nothing one could say she hadn't done—one's perception could bear only on what she hadn't become; so that, as he thus perceived, though she might have affected Europe even as she now affecting *him*, she was a pure negation of its having affected herself, unless perhaps by adding to her power to make him feel how little he could impose on her.

THE IVORY TOWER, Book 2, Chapter 1

Lord Petherton

Lord Petherton, a man of five-and-thirty, whose robust but symmetrical proportions gave to his dark blue double-breasted coat an air of tightness that just failed of compromising his tailor, had for his main facial sign a certain pleasant brutality, the effect partly of a bold handsome parade of carnivorous teeth, partly of an expression of nose suggesting that this feature had paid a little, in the heat of youth, for some aggression at the time admired and even publicly commemorated. He would have been ugly, he substantively granted, had he not been happy; he would have been dangerous had he not been warranted. Many things doubtless performed for him this last service, but none so much as the delightful sound of his voice, the voice, as it were, of another man, a nature reclaimed, supercivilized, adjusted to the perpetual "chaff" which kept him smiling in a way that would have been a mistake and indeed an impossibility if he had really been witty. His bright familiarity was that of a young prince whose confidence had never had to falter, and the only thing that at all qualified the resemblance was the equal familiarity excited in his subjects.

THE AWKWARD AGE, Book 2, Chapter 4

The Countess Gemini

In reality Isabel would as soon have thought of despising her as of passing a moral judgement on a grasshopper. She was not indifferent to her husband's sister, however; she was rather a little afraid of her. She wondered at her; she thought her very extraordinary. The Countess seemed to her to have no soul; she was like a bright rare shell, with a polished surface and a remarkably pink lip, in which something would rattle when you shook it. This rattle was apparently the Countess's spiritual principle, a little loose nut that tumbled about inside of her. She was too odd for disdain, too anomalous for comparisons.

THE PORTRAIT OF A LADY, Chapter 44

Merton Densher

He was in short visibly absent-minded, irregularly clever, liable to drop what was near and to take up what was far; he was more a respecter, in general, than a follower of custom. He suggested above all, however, that wondrous state of youth in which the elements, the metals more or less precious, are so in fusion and fermentation that the question of the final stamp, the pressure that fixes the value, must wait for comparative coolness.

THE WINGS OF THE DOVE, Chapter 3

Madame Merle

When Madame Merle was neither writing, nor painting, nor touching the piano, she was usually employed upon wonderful tasks of rich embroidery, cushions, curtains, decorations for the chimney-piece; an art in which her bold, free invention was as noted as the agility of her needle. She was never idle, for when engaged in none of the ways I have mentioned she was either reading (she appeared to Isabel to read "everything important"), or walking out, or playing patience with the cards, or talking with her fellow inmates. And with all this she had always the social quality, was never rudely absent and yet never too seated. She laid down her pastimes as easily as she took them up; she worked and talked at the same time, and appeared to impute scant worth to anything she did. She gave away her sketches and tapestries; she rose from the piano or remained there, according to the convenience of her auditors, which she always unerringly divined. She was in short the most comfortable, profitable, amenable person to live with.

THE PORTRAIT OF A LADY, Chapter 46

Fannie Assingham

She had in her life two great holes to fill, and she described herself as dropping social scraps into them as she had known old ladies, in her early American time, drop morsels of silk into the baskets in which they collected the material for some eventual patchwork quilt. One of these gaps in Mrs. Assingham's completeness was her want of children; the other was her want of wealth. It was wonderful how little either, in the fulness of time, came to show; sympathy and curiosity could render their objects practically filial, just as an English husband who in his military years had "run" everything in his regiment could make economy blossom like the rose.

THE GOLDEN BOWL, Chapter 3

Prince Amerigo

He had stood still, at many a moment of the previous month, with the thought, freshly determined or renewed, of the general expectation—to define it roughly—of which he was the subject. What was singular was that it seemed not so much an expectation of anything in particular as a large bland blank assumption of merits almost beyond notation, of essential quality and value. It was as if he had been some old embossed coin, of a purity of gold no longer used, stamped with glorious arms, mediaeval, wonderful, of which the "worth" in mere modern change, sovereigns and half-crowns, would be great enough, but as to which, since there were finer ways of using it, such taking to pieces was superfluous. That was the image for the security in which it was open to him to rest; he was to constitute a possession, yet was to escape being reduced to his component parts.

THE GOLDEN BOWL, Chapter 1

Aggie and Nanda Brookenham

Little Aggie differed from any young person he had ever met in that she had been deliberately prepared for consumption and in that furthermore the gentleness of her spirit had immensely helped the preparation. Nanda, beside her, was a Northern savage, and the reason was partly that the elements of that young lady's nature were already, were publicly, were almost indecorously active. They were practically there for good or for ill; experience was still to come and what they might work out to still a mystery; but the sum would get itself done with the figures now on the slate. On little Aggie's slate the figures were yet to be written; which sufficiently accounted for the difference of the two surfaces. Both the girls struck him as lambs with the great shambles of life in their future; but while one, with its neck in a pink ribbon, had no consciousness but that of being fed from the hand with the small sweet biscuit of unobjectionable knowledge, the other struggled with instincts and forebodings, with the suspicion of its doom and the far-borne scent, in the flowery fields, of blood.

THE AWKWARD AGE, Book 5, Chapter 3

Mrs. Saltram

It was of course familiar to me that Saltram was incapable of keeping the engagements which, after their separation, he had entered into with regard to his wife, a deeply wronged, justly resentful, quite irreproachable and insufferable person. She often appeared at my chambers to talk over his lapses; for if, as she declared, she had washed her hands of him, she had carefully preserved the water of this ablution, which she handed about for analysis. She had arts of her own of exciting one's impatience, the most infallible of which was perhaps her assumption that we were kind to her because we liked her. In reality her personal fall had been a sort of social rise—since I had seen the moments when, in our little conscientious circle, her desolation almost made her the fashion.

THE COXON FUND, Chapter 4

Isabel Archer

It often seemed to her that she thought too much about herself; you could have made her colour, any day in the year, by calling her a rank egoist. She was always planning out her development, desiring her perfection, observing her progress. Her nature had, in her conceit, a certain garden-like quality, a suggestion of perfume and murmuring boughs, of shady bowers and lengthening vistas, which made her feel that introspection was, after all, an exercise in the open air, and that a visit to the recesses of one's spirit was harmless when one returned from it with a lapful of roses.

> THE PORTRAIT OF A LADY, Chapter 6

Gilbert Osmond (1)

His good-humour was imperturbable, his knowledge of the right fact, his production of the right word, as convenient as the friendly flicker of a match for your cigarette. Clearly he was amused—as amused as a man could be who was so little ever surprised, and that made him almost applausive. It was not that his spirits were visibly high—he would never, in the concert of pleasure, touch the big drum by so much as a knuckle: he had a mortal dislike to the high, ragged note, to what he called random ravings. He thought Miss Archer sometimes of too precipitate a readiness. It was pity she had that fault, because if she had not had it she would really have had none; she would have been as smooth to his general need of her as handled ivory to the palm. If he was not personally loud, however, he was deep, and during these closing days of the Roman May he knew a complacency that matched with slow irregular walks under the pines of the Villa Borghese, among the small sweet meadow-flowers and the mossy marbles.

THE PORTRAIT OF A LADY, Chapter 29

Gilbert Osmond (2)

The desire to have something or other to show for his "parts"—to show somehow or other—had been the dream of his youth; but as the years went on the conditions attached to any marked proof of rarity had affected him more and more as gross and detestable; like the swallowing of mugs of beer to advertise what one could "stand." If an anonymous drawing on a museum wall had been conscious and watchful it might have known this peculiar pleasure of being at last and all of a sudden identified—as from the hand of a great master—by the so high and so unnoticed fact of style. His "style" was what the girl had discovered with a little help; and now, beside herself enjoying it, she should publish it to the world without his having any of the trouble.

THE PORTRAIT OF A LADY, Chapter 29

Mr. Mudge, the Grocer

He had, at any rate, ceased to be all day long in her eyes, and this left something a little fresh for them to rest on of a Sunday. During the three months that he had remained at Cocker's after her consent to their engagement, she had often asked herself what it was that marriage would be able to add to a familiarity so final. Opposite there, behind the counter of which his superior stature, his whiter apron, his more clustering curls and more present, too present, h's had been for a couple of years the principal ornament, he had moved to and fro before her as on the small sanded floor of their contracted future.

IN THE CAGE, Chapter 1

Gilbert Osmond (3)

His tastes, his studies, his accomplishments, his collections, were all for a purpose. His life on his hill-top at Florence had been the conscious attitude of years. His solitude, his ennui, his love for his daughter, his good manners, his bad manners, were so many features of a mental image constantly present to him as a model of impertinence and mystification. His ambition was not to please the world, but to please himself by exciting the world's curiosity and then declining to satisfy it. It had made him feel great, ever, to play the world a trick.

THE PORTRAIT OF A LADY, Chapter 39

Things

Madame Merle's Credo

"I don't care anything about his house," said Isabel.

"That's very crude of you. When you've lived as long as I you'll see that every human being has his shell and that you must take the shell into account. By the shell I mean the whole envelope of circumstances. There's no such thing as an isolated man or woman; we're each of us made up of some cluster of appurtenances. What shall we call our 'self?' Where does it begin? where does it end? It overflows into everything that belongs to us—and then it flows back again. I know a large part of myself is in the clothes I choose to wear. I've a great respect for *things*! One's self—for other people—is one's expression of one's self; and one's house, one's furniture, one's garments, the books one reads, the company one keeps—these things are all expressive."

THE PORTRAIT OF A LADY, Chapter 19

Miss Gostrey's Flat

Her compact and crowded little chambers, almost dusky, as they at first struck him, with accumulations, represented a supreme general adjustment to opportunities and conditions. Wherever he looked he saw an old ivory or an old brocade, and he scarce knew where to sit for fear of a misappliance. The life of the occupant struck him of a sudden as more charged with possession even than Chad's or than Miss Barrace's; wide as his glimpse had lately become of the empire of "things," what was before him still enlarged it; the lust of the eyes and the pride of life had indeed thus their temple. It was the innermost nook of the shrine—as brown as a pirate's cave. In the brownness were glints of gold; patches of purple were in the gloom; objects all that caught, through the muslin, with their high rarity, the light of the low windows. Nothing was clear about them but that they were precious, and they brushed his ignorance with their contempt as a flower, in a liberty taken with him, might have been whisked under his nose.

THE AMBASSADORS, Book 3, Chapter 2

Madame de Vionnet's "Things"

Chad and Miss Gostrey had rummaged and purchased and picked up and exchanged, sifting, selecting, comparing; whereas the mistress of the scene before him, beautifully passive under the spell of transmission—transmission from her father's line, he quite made up his mind—had only received, accepted and been quiet. When she hadn't been quiet she had been moved at the most to some occult charity for some fallen fortune. There had been objects she or her predecessors might even conceivably have parted with under need, but Strether couldn't suspect them of having sold old pieces to get "better" ones. They would have felt no difference as to better or worse. He could but imagine their having felt—perhaps in emigration, in proscription, for his sketch was slight and confused—the pressure of want or the obligation of sacrifice.

THE AMBASSADORS, Book 6, Chapter 1

The Old Bachelor's House

Everything at Mr. Carteret's appeared to Nick to be on a larger scale than anywhere else—the tea-cups, the knives and forks, the door-handles, the chair-backs, the legs of mutton, the candles and the lumps of coal: they represented and apparently exhausted the master's sense of pleasing effect, for the house was not otherwise decorated. Nick thought it really hideous, but he was capable at the same time of extracting a degree of amusement from anything that was strongly characteristic, and Mr. Carteret's interior expressed a whole view of life. Our young man was generous enough to find a hundred instructive intimations in it even at the time it came over him (as it always did at Beauclere) that this was the view he himself was expected to take.

THE TRAGIC MUSE, Chapter 26

The Horrors of "Waterbath"

It was an ugliness fundamental and systematic, the result of the abnormal nature of the Brigstocks, from whose composition the principle of taste had been extravagantly omitted. In the arrangement of their home some other principle, remarkably active, but uncanny and obscure, had operated instead, with consequences depressing to behold, consequences that took the form of a universal futility. The house was bad in all conscience, but it might have passed if they had only let it alone. This saving mercy was beyond them; they had smothered it with trumpery ornament and scrapbook art, with strange excrescences and bunchy draperies, with gimcracks that might have been keepsakes for maid-servants and nondescript conveniences that might have been prizes for the blind.

THE SPOILS OF POYNTON, Chapter 1

The Glories of "Poynton"

They went at last, the wiseheads, down to Poynton, where the palpitating girl had the full revelation. "*Now* do you know how I feel?" Mrs. Gereth asked when in the wonderful hall, three minutes after their arrival, her pretty associate dropped on a seat with a soft gasp and a roll of dilated eyes. The answer came clearly enough, and in the rapture of that first walk through the house Fleda took a prodigious span. She perfectly understood how Mrs. Gereth felt—she had understood but meagrely before, and the two women embraced with tears over the tightening of their bond—tears which on the younger one's part were the natural and usual sign of her submission to perfect beauty.

THE SPOILS OF POYNTON, Chapter 3

"Aunt Maud" Lowder's House at Lancaster Gate

It was manifest they [the furnishings] were splendid and were furthermore conclusively British. They constituted an order and they abounded in rare material—precious woods, metals, stuffs, stones. He had never dreamed of anything so fringed and scalloped, so buttoned and corded, drawn everywhere so tight, and curled everywhere so thick. He had never dreamed of so much gilt and glass, so much satin and plush, so much rosewood and marble and malachite. But it was, above all, the solid forms, the wasted finish, the misguided cost, the general attestation of morality and money, a good conscience and a big balance.

THE WINGS OF THE DOVE, Chapter 4

The Actress's Parlor

Gabriel Nash wandered about the room, looking at the votive offerings which converted the little panelled box, decorated in sallow white and gold, into a theatrical museum: the presents, the portraits, the wreaths, the diadems, the letters, framed and glazed, the trophies and tributes and relics collected by Madame Carré during half a century of renown. The profusion of this testimony was hardly more striking than the confession of something missed, something hushed, which seemed to rise from it all and make it melancholy, like a reference to clappings which, in the nature of things, could now only be present as a silence: so that if the place was full of history, it was the form without the fact, or at the most a redundancy of the one to a pinch of the other—the history of a mask, of a squeak, a record of movements in the air.

THE TRAGIC MUSE, Chapter 7

Madame de Vionnet's Interior (1)

She occupied, his hostess, in the Rue de Bellechasse, the first floor of an old house to which our visitors had had access from an old clean court. The court was large and open, full of revelations, for our friend, of the habit of privacy, the peace of intervals, the dignity of distances and approaches; the house, to his restless sense, was in the high homely style of an elder day, and the ancient Paris that he was always looking for—sometimes intensely felt, sometimes more acutely missed—was in the immemorial polish of the wide waxed staircase and in the fine *boiseries*, the medallions, mouldings, mirrors, great clear spaces, of the greyish-white salon into which he had been shown. He found himself making out, as a background of the occupant, some glory, some prosperity of the First Empire, some Napoleonic glamour, some dim lustre of the great legend; elements clinging still to all the consular chairs and mythological brasses and sphinxes' heads and faded surfaces of satin striped with alternate silk.

THE AMBASSADORS, Book 6, Chapter 1

Gardencourt

The day was dark and cold; the dusk was thick in the corners of the wide brown rooms. The house was perfectly still—with a stillness that Isabel remembered; it had filled all the place for days before the death of her uncle. She left the drawing-room and wandered about—strolled into the library and along the gallery of pictures, where, in the deep silence, her footstep made an echo. Nothing was changed; she recognised everything she had seen years before; it might have been only yesterday she had stood there. She envied the security of valuable "pieces" which change by no hair's breadth, only grow in value, while their owners lose inch by inch youth, happiness, beauty.

THE PORTRAIT OF A LADY, Chapter 54

Dialogues

Daisy Is Warned by Mrs. Walker

"Do get in and drive round *with* me," Mrs. Walker pleaded.

"That would be charming, but it's so fascinating just as I am!"—with which the girl radiantly took in the gentlemen on either side of her.

"It may be fascinating, dear child, but it's not the custom here," urged the lady of the victoria, leaning forward in this vehicle with her hands devoutly clasped.

"Well, it ought to be then!" Daisy imperturbably laughed. "If I didn't walk I'd expire."

"You're old enough to be more reasonable. You're old enough, dear Miss Miller, to be talked about."

Daisy wondered to extravagance. "Talked about? What do you mean?"

"Come into my carriage and I'll tell you."

Daisy turned shining eyes again from one of the gentlemen beside her to the other. "I don't think I want to know what you mean," the girl presently said. "I don't think I should like it."

DAISY MILLER, Chapter 3

Newman and Madame de Bellegarde (1)

Valentin presented his friend, and Newman came sufficiently near to the old lady by the fire to take in that she would offer him no handshake—so that he knew he had the air of waiting, and a little like a customer in a shop, to see what she *would* offer. He received a rapid impression of a white, delicate, aged face, with a high forehead, a small mouth and a pair of cold blue eyes which had kept much of the clearness of youth.

"I ought to have seen you before," said Madame de Bellegarde. "You've paid several visits to my daughter."

"Oh, yes," Newman liberally smiled; "Madame de Cintré and I are old friends by this time."

"You've gone very fast," she went on.

"Not so fast as I should like."

"Ah, you're very ambitious," the old woman returned.

"Well, if I don't know what I want by this time I suppose I never shall."

Madame de Bellegarde looked at him with her cold fine eyes.

"I'm very ambitious too," she said.

THE AMERICAN, Chapter 10

Newman and Madame de Bellegarde (2)

"Your daughter's very beautiful," he said at last.

"She's very perverse," the old woman returned.

"I'm glad to hear it," he smiled. "It makes me hope."

"Hope what?"

"That she'll consent some day to marry me."

She slowly got up. "That really is your 'great idea?'"

"Yes. Will you give it any countenance?"

Madame de Bellegarde looked at him hard and shook her head. "No!"

"Will you then just let me alone with my chance?"

"You don't know what you ask. I'm a very proud and meddlesome old person."

"Well, I'm very rich," he returned with a world of desperate intention.

She fixed her eyes on the floor, and he thought it probable she was weighing the reasons in favour of resenting his so calculated directness. But at last looking up, "How rich?" she simply articulated.

> THE AMERICAN, Chapter 10

The Salon

"Did you ever see such a dreadful place?"

Sherringham stared. "Aren't the things good? I had an idea—"

"Good?" cried Lady Agnes. "They're too odious, too wicked."

"Ah," said Peter, laughing, "that's what people fall into, if they live abroad. The French oughtn't to live abroad."

THE TRAGIC MUSE, Chapter 3

Strether Tries to Explain Mrs. Newsome to Miss Gostrey

"They're very busy people and Mrs. Newsome in particular has a large full life. She's moreover highly nervous—and not at all strong."

"You mean she's an American invalid?"

He carefully distinguished. "There's nothing she likes less than to be called one, but she would consent to be one of those things, I think," he laughed, "if it were the only way to be the other."

"Consent to be an American in order to be an invalid?"

"No," said Strether, "the other way round. She's at any rate delicate sensitive high-strung. She puts so much of herself into everything—"

Ah Maria knew these things! "That she has nothing left for anything else? Of course she hasn't."

THE AMBASSADORS, Book 2, Chapter 1

Women's Rights

"God forbid, madam! I consider women have no business to be reasonable."

His companion turned upon him, slowly and mildly, and each of her glasses, in her aspect of reproach, had the glitter of an enormous tear. "Do you regard us, then, simply as lovely baubles?" The effect of this question, as coming from Miss Birdseye, and referring in some degree to her own venerable identity, was such as to move him to irresistible laughter.

THE BOSTONIANS, Chapter 23

Chad Newsome in Paris

"Chad's a rare case!" he luminously observed. "He's awfully changed," he added.

"Then you see it too?"

"The way he has improved? Oh yes—I think every one must see it. But I'm not sure," said little Bilham, "that I did n't like him about as well in his other state."

"Then this *is* really a new state altogether?"

"Well," the young man after a moment returned. "I'm not sure he was really meant by nature to be quite so good. It's like the new edition of an old book that one has been fond of—revised and amended, brought up to date, but not quite the thing one knew and loved."

THE AMBASSADOR, Book 4, Chapter 2

Isabel and Her Aunt

"Of course you're vexed at my interfering with you," said Mrs. Touchett.

Isabel considered. "I'm not vexed, but I'm surprised—and a good deal mystified. Wasn't it proper I should remain in the drawing-room?"

'Not in the least. Young girls here—in decent houses—don't sit alone with the gentlemen late at night."

"You were very right to tell me then," said Isabel. "I don't understand it, but I'm very glad to know it."

"I shall always tell you," her aunt answered, "whenever I see you taking what seems to me too much liberty."

"Pray do, but I don't say I shall always think your remonstrance just."

"Very likely not. You're too fond of your own ways."

"Yes, I think I'm very fond of them. But I always want to know the things one shouldn't do."

"So as to do them?" asked her aunt.

"So as to choose," said Isabel.

THE PORTRAIT OF A LADY, Chapter 7

Mrs. Touchett Learns of Isabel's Engagement

"What *you* will marry for, heaven only knows. People usually marry as they go into partnership—to set up a house. But in your partnership you'll bring everything."

"Is it that Mr. Osmond isn't rich? Is that what you're talking about?" Isabel asked.

"He has no money; he has no name; he has no importance. I value such things and I have the courage to say it; I think they're very precious. Many other people think the same, and they show it. But they give some other reason."

Isabel hesitated a little. "I think I value everything that's valuable. I care very much for money, and that's why I wish Mr. Osmond to have a little."

"Give it to him then; but marry some one else."

THE PORTRAIT OF A LADY, Chapter 33

English Hours

The English

They didn't like *les situations nettes*—that was all he was very sure of. They wouldn't have them at any price; it had been their national genius and their national success to avoid them at every point. They called it themselves, with complacency, their wonderful spirit of compromise—the very influence of which actually so hung about him here from moment to moment that the earth and the air, the light and the colour, the fields and the hills and the sky, the blue-green counties and the cold cathedrals, owed to it every accent of their tone. Verily, as one had to feel in presence of such a picture, it had succeeded; it had made, up to now, for that seated solidity in the rich sea-mist on which the garish, the supposedly envious, peoples have ever cooled their eyes. But it was at the same time precisely why even much initiation left one at given moments so puzzled as to the element of staleness in all the freshness and of freshness in all the staleness, of innocence in the guilt and of guilt in the innocence.

THE GOLDEN BOWL, Chapter 22

London in the 1850s (1)

The London people had for themselves, at the same time, an exuberance of type; we found it in particular a world of costume, often of very odd costume—the most intimate notes of which were the postmen in their frock-coats of military red and their black beaver hats; the milkwomen, in hats that often emulated these, in little shawls and strange short, full frocks, revealing enormous boots, with their pails swung from their shoulders on wooden yokes; the inveterate footmen hooked behind the coaches of the rich, frequently in pairs and carrying staves, together with the mounted and belted grooms without the attendance of whom riders, of whichever sex—and riders then were much more numerous—almost never went forth.

A SMALL BOY AND OTHERS, Chapter 22

London in the 1850s (2)

The range of character, on the other hand, reached rather dreadfully down; there were embodied and exemplified "horrors" in the streets beside which any present exhibition is pale, and I well remember the almost terrified sense of their salience produced in me a couple of years later, on the occasion of a flying return from the Continent with my father, by a long, an interminable drive westward from the London Bridge railway-station. It was a soft June evening, with a lingering light and swarming crowds, as they then seemed to me, of figures reminding me of George Cruikshank's Artful Dodger and his Bill Sikes and his Nancy, only with the bigger brutality of life, which pressed upon the cab, the early-Victorian fourwheeler, as we jogged over the Bridge, and cropped up in more and more gas-lit patches for all our course, culminating, somewhere far to the west, in the vivid picture, framed by the cab-window, of a woman reeling backward as a man felled her to the ground with a blow in the face.

A SMALL BOY AND OTHERS, Chapter 22

The English Prison

It looked very sinister and wicked, to Miss Pynsent's eyes, and she wondered why a prison should have such an evil air if it was erected in the interest of justice and order—a builded protest, precisely, against vice and villainy. This particular penitentiary struck her as about as bad and wrong as those who were in it; it threw a blight on the face of day, making the river seem foul and poisonous and the opposite bank, with a protrusion of long-necked chimneys, unsightly gasometers and deposits of rubbish, wear the aspect of a region at whose expense the jail had been populated.

THE PRINCESS CASAMASSIMA, Chapter 3

Captain Sholto

Sholto was a curious and not particularly edifying English type, as the Princess further described him; one of those odd figures produced by old societies that have run to seed, corrupt and exhausted civilisations. He was a cumberer of the earth—purely selfish for all his devoted disinterested airs. He was nothing whatever in himself and had no character or merit save by tradition, reflexion, imitation, superstition. He had a longish pedigree—he came of some musty mouldy "county family," people with a local reputation and an immense lack of general importance; he had taken the greatest care of his little fortune. He had travelled all over the globe several times, "for the shooting," in that murdering ravaging way of the English, the destruction, the extirpation of creatures more beautiful, more soaring and more nimble than themselves. He had a little taste, a little cleverness, a little reading, a little good furniture, a little French and Italian (he exaggerated these latter quantities), an immense deal of assurance and unmitigated leisure.

THE PRINCESS CASAMASSIMA, Chapter 5

The Dinner Party

The entertainment offered a few evenings before Easter, and at which Maggie and he were inevitably present as guests, was a discharge of obligations not insistently incurred, and had thus possibly all the more the note of this almost Arcadian optimism: a large bright dull murmurous mild-eyed middle-aged dinner, involving for the most part very bland, though very exalted, immensely announceable and hierarchically placeable couples.

THE GOLDEN BOWL, Chapter 19

The House Party (1)

What any one "thought" of any one else—above all of any one else *with* any one else—was a matter incurring in these halls so little awkward formulation that hovering Judgement, the spirit with the scales, might perfectly have been imaged there as some rather snubbed and subdued but quite trained and tactful poor relation, of equal, of the properest, lineage, only of aspect a little dingy, doubtless from too limited a change of dress, for whose tacit and abstemious presence, never betrayed by a rattle of her rusty machine, a room in the attic and a plate at the side table were decently usual.

THE GOLDEN BOWL, Chapter 20

A Young Lady

"The lady with whom you were so good as to make me acquainted is a beautiful specimen of the English garden-flower, the product of high cultivation and much tending; a tall, delicate stem, with the head set upon it in a manner which, as I recall it, is distinctly so much to the good in my day. She's the perfect type of the object *raised*, or bred, and everything about her is homogeneous, from the angle of her elbow to the way she drops that vague, conventional, dry little "Oh!" which dispenses with all further performance. That sort of completeness is always satisfying. But I didn't satisfy her, and she didn't understand me. I don't think they usually understand."

THE TRAGIC MUSE, Chapter 9

The Garden

The ordered English garden, in the freshness of the day, was delightful to Strether, who liked the sound, under his feet, of the tight fine gravel, packed with the chronic damp, and who had the idlest eye for the deep smoothness of turf and the clean curves of paths.

THE AMBASSADOR, Book 1, Chapter 3

The House Party (2)
The Dinner Hour

This especial hour, at Newmarch, had always a splendour that asked little of interpretation, that even carried itself, with an amiable arrogance, as indifferent to what the imagination could do for it. I think the imagination, in those halls of art and fortune, was almost inevitably accounted a poor matter; the whole place and its participants abounded so in pleasantness and picture, in all the felicities, for every sense, taken for granted there by the very basis of life, that even the sense most finely poetic, aspiring to extract the moral, could scarce have helped feeling itself treated to something of the snub that affects—when it does affect—the uninvited reporter in whose face a door is closed. I said to myself during dinner that these were scenes in which a transcendent intelligence had after all no application, and that, in short, any preposterous acuteness might easily suffer among them such a loss of dignity as overtakes the newspaper-man kicked out. We existed, all of us together, to be handsome and happy, to be really what we looked—since we looked tremendously well; to be that and neither more nor less, so not discrediting by musty secrets and aggressive doubts our high privilege of harmony and taste.

THE SACRED FOUNT, Chapter 9

The Artist in Britain

Overt, who had spent a considerable part of his short life in foreign lands, made now, but not for the first time, the reflexion that whereas in those countries he had almost always recognised the artist and the man of letters by his personal "type," the mould of his face, the character of his head, the expression of his figure, and even the indications of his dress, so in England this identification was as little as possible a matter of course, thanks to the greater conformity, the habit of sinking the profession instead of advertising it, the general diffusion of the air of the gentleman—the gentleman committed to no particular set of ideas.

THE LESSON OF THE MASTER

The Doctor in Harley Street (1)

What it really came to, on the morrow, was that the great man had, a little, to excuse himself; had, by a rare accident—for he kept his consulting-hours in general rigorously free—but ten minutes to give her; ten mere minutes which he yet placed at her service in a manner that she admired even more than she could meet it: so crystal-clean the great empty cup of attention that he set between them on the table.

THE WINGS OF THE DOVE, Chapter 12

The Doctor in Harley Street (2)

Wanting to know more about a patient than how a patient was constructed or deranged couldn't be, even on the part of the greatest of doctors, anything but some form or other of the desire to let the patient down easily. When that was the case the reason, in turn, could only be, too manifestly, pity; and when pity held up its tell-tale face like a head on a pike, in a French revolution, bobbing before a window, what was the inference but that the patient was bad?

THE WINGS OF THE DOVE, Chapter 12

Chester

The tortuous wall—girdle, long since snapped, of the little swollen city, half held in place by careful civic hands—wanders in narrow file between parapets smoothed by peaceful generations, pausing here and there for a dismantled gate or a bridged gap, with rises and drops, steps up and steps down, queer twists, queer contacts, peeps into homely streets and under the brows of gables, views of cathedral tower and waterside fields, of huddled English town and ordered English country. Too deep almost for words was the delight of these things to Strether; yet as deeply mixed with it were certain images of his inward picture. He had trod this walk in the far-off time, at twenty-five; but that, instead of spoiling it, only enriched it for present feeling and marked his renewal as a thing substantial enough to share.

THE AMBASSADORS, Book 1, Chapter 1

Shakespeare's Birthplace

The shrine at which he was to preside—though he had always lacked occasion to approach it—figured to him as the most sacred known to the steps of men, the early home of the supreme poet, the Mecca of the English-speaking race. He felt as if a window had opened into a great green woodland, a woodland that had a name all glorious, immortal, that was peopled with vivid figures, each of them renowned, and that gave out a murmur, deep as the sound of the sea, which was the rustle in forest shade of all the poetry, the beauty, the colour of life.

THE BIRTHPLACE

The Exotic Author

The lady who had been sitting with Mrs. Ambient was a jolly ruddy personage in velveteen and limp feathers, whom I guessed to be the vicar's wife—our hostess didn't introduce me—and who immediately began to talk to Ambient about chrysanthemums. This was a safe subject, and yet there was a certain surprise for me in seeing the author of "Beltraffio" even in such superficial communion with the Church of England. His writings implied so much detachment from that institution, expressed a view of life so profane, as it were, so independent and so little likely in general to be thought edifying, that I should have expected to find him an object of horror to vicars and their ladies—of horror repaid on his own part by any amount of effortless derision. This proved how little I knew as yet of the English people and their extraordinary talent for keeping up their forms.

THE AUTHOR OF "BELTRAFFIO"

Maisie's Governesses

If she knew her instructress was poor and queer she also knew she was not nearly so "qualified" as Miss Overmore, who could say lots of dates straight off (letting you hold the book yourself), state the position of Malabar, play six pieces without notes and, in a sketch, put in beautifully the trees and houses and difficult parts. Maisie herself could play more pieces than Mrs. Wix, who was moreover visibly ashamed of her houses and trees and could only, with the help of a smutty forefinger, of doubtful legitimacy in the field of art, do the smoke coming out of the chimneys.

WHAT MAISIE KNEW, Chapter 4

The English Village

All this would be a part of the suggestion of leisure that invariably descended upon him at Beauclere—the image of a sloping shore where the tide of time broke with a ripple too faint to be a warning. But there was another admonition that was almost equally sure to descend upon his spirit in a summer hour, in a stroll about the grand abbey, to sink into it as the light lingered on the rough red walls and the local accent of the children sounded soft in the churchyard. It was simply the sense of England—a sort of apprehended revelation of his country. The dim annals of the place appeared to be in the air (foundations bafflingly early, a great monastic life, wars of the Roses, with battles and blood in the streets, and then the long quietude of the respectable centuries, all cornfields and magistrates and vicars), and these things were connected with an emotion that arose from the green country, the rich land so infinitely lived in, and laid on him a hand that was too ghostly to press and yet somehow too urgent to be light.

THE TRAGIC MUSE, Chapter 16

Millicent Henning

She was to her blunt, expanded finger-tips a daughter of London, of the crowded streets and bustling traffic of the great city; she had drawn her health and strength from its dingy courts and foggy thoroughfares and peopled its parks and squares and crescents with her ambitions; it had entered into her blood and her bone, the sound of her voice and the carriage of her head; she understood it by instinct and loved it with passion; she represented its immense vulgarities and curiosities, its brutality and its knowingness, its good-nature and its impudence, and might have figured, in an allegorical procession, as a kind of glorified townswoman, a nymph of the wilderness of Middlesex, a flower of the clustered parishes, the genius of urban civilisation, the muse of cockneyism.

THE PRINCESS CASAMASSIMA, Chapter 4

Bly

The summer had turned, the summer had gone; the autumn had dropped upon Bly and had blown out half our lights. The place with its grey sky and withered garlands, its bared spaces and scattered dead leaves, was like a theatre after the performance—all strewn with crumpled playbills.

THE TURN OF THE SCREW, Chapter 13

Paintings

Strether's Lambinet

Romance could weave itself, for Strether's sense, out of elements mild enough; and he could thrill a little at the chance of seeing something somewhere that would remind him of a certain small Lambinet that had charmed him, long years before, at a Boston dealer's and that he had quite absurdly never forgotten. It had been offered, he remembered, at a price he had been instructed to believe the lowest ever named for a Lambinet, a price he had never felt so poor as on having to recognise, all the same, as beyond a dream of possibility. He had dreamed—had turned and twisted possibilities for an hour: it had been the only adventure of his life in connexion with the purchase of a work of art. The adventure, it will be perceived, was modest; but the memory, beyond all reason and by some accident of association, was sweet. The little Lambinet abode with him as the picture he *would* have bought—the particular production that had made him for the moment overstep the modesty of nature. He was quite aware that if he were to see it again he should perhaps have a drop or a shock, and he never found himself wishing that the wheel of time would turn it up again, just as he had seen it in the maroon-coloured, sky-lighted inner shrine of Tremont Street.

THE AMBASSADORS, Book 11, Chapter 3

The Faceless Portrait

This work, prominent in its place over the mantel, depicted a personage who simply appeared to have sought to ignore our friend's appeal by turning away his face. This it was that constituted the prodigy, for Ralph had truly never seen a gentleman painted, and painted beautifully, in so thankless a posture. It gave the figure a conscious air which might have made for ridicule had it not so positively made for life: whereby to laugh at it would verily have been, in spite of its averted look, too much like laughing in a gentleman's face. The gentleman in question here had turned his back, and for all the world as if he had turned it *within* the picture. This of course was far from the first time Ralph had admired and studied him, but it was the first time of his finding his attention throb with the idea that the actual attitude might change—that it had even probably, that it had in fact repeatedly, done so. Extravagant enough such an imagination, but now settling on our young man in force—the prodigy that when one wasn't there the figure looked as figures in portraits inveterately look, somewhere into the room, and that this miraculous shift, the concealment of feature and identity, took place only when one's step drew near.

THE SENSE OF THE PAST, Book 2

Meissonier's "Friedland"

It is hard, however, to admire it restrictively without seeming to admire it less than one really does. It seems to me it is a thing of parts rather than an interesting whole. The parts are admirable, and the more you analyse them the better they seem. The best thing, say, is a certain cuirassier, and in the cuirassier the best thing is his clothes, and in his clothes the best thing is his leather straps, and in his leather straps the best thing is the buckles. This is the kind of work you find yourself performing over the picture; you may go on indefinitely. That great general impression which, first and foremost, it is the duty of an excellent picture to give you, seems to me to be wanting here. M. Meissonier is the great archaeologist of the Napoleonic era; he understands to a buttonhole the uniform of the Grand Army.

PARISIAN SKETCHES

Lady Beldonald

She is a person whom vanity has had the odd effect of keeping positively safe and sound—it has kept her from the first moment of full consciousness, one feels, exactly in the same place. It has protected her from every danger, has made her absolutely proper and prim. If she is "preserved," it is her vanity that has beautifully done it—putting her years ago in a plate-glass case and closing up the receptacle against every breath of air. How shouldn't she be preserved, when you might smash your knuckles on this transparency before you could crack it? And she *is*—oh, amazingly! Preservation is scarce the word for the rare condition of her surface. She looks *naturally* new, as if she took out every night her large, lovely, varnished eyes and put them in water. The thing was to paint her, I perceived, *in* the glass case—a most tempting, attaching feat; render to the full the shining, interposing plate and the general show-window effect.

THE BELDONALD HOLBEIN

Faces and Figures

Prince Amerigo

The Prince's dark blue eyes were of the finest and, on occasion, precisely, resembled nothing so much as the high windows of a Roman palace, of an historic front by one of the great old designers, thrown open on a feast-day to the golden air.

THE GOLDEN BOWL, Chapter 2

Lawyer Crick

His domestic companion of these days again and again struck him as most touching the point at issue, and that point alone, when most proclaiming at every pore that there wasn't difference, in all the world, between one thing and another. The refusal of his whole person to figure as a fact invidiously distinguishable, that of his aspect to have an identity, of his eyes to have a consciousness, of his hair to have a colour, of his nose to have a form, of his mouth to have a motion, of his voice to consent to any separation of sounds, made intercourse with him at once extremely easy and extraordinarily empty; it was deprived of the flicker of anything by the way and resembled the act of moving forward in a perfectly-rolling carriage with the blind of each window neatly drawn down.

THE IVORY TOWER, Book 4, Chapter 1

Lady Aurora

Her clothes looked as if she had worn them a good deal in the rain, and the note of a certain disrepair in her apparel was given by a hole in one of her black gloves, through which a white finger gleamed. She was plain and different and she might have been poor; but in the fine grain and sloping, shrinking slimness of her whole person, the delicacy of her curious features and a kind of cultivated quality in her sweet, vague, civil expression, there was a suggestion of race, of long transmission, of an organism that had resulted from fortunate touch after touch. She was not a common woman; she was one of the caprices of an aristocracy.

> THE PRINCESS CASAMASSIMA, Chapter 8

Madame Carré

The old actress presented herself to a casual glance as a red-faced woman in a wig, with beady eyes, a hooked nose and pretty hands; but Nick Dormer, who had a perception of physiognomy, speedily observed that these free characteristics included a great deal of delicate detail—an eyebrow, a nostril, a flitting of expressions, as if a multitude of little facial wires were pulled from within. This accomplished artist had in particular a mouth which was visibly a rare instrument, a pair of lips whose curves and fine corners spoke of a lifetime of "points" unerringly made and verses exquisitely spoken, helping to explain the purity of the sound that issued from them. Her whole countenance had the look of long service—of a thing infinitely worn and used, drawn and stretched to excess, with its elasticity overdone and its springs relaxed, yet religiously preserved and kept in repair, like an old valuable time-piece, which might have quivered and rumbled, but could be trusted to strike the hour.

THE TRAGIC MUSE, Chapter 7

Horton ("Haughty") Vint

His features, after a manner of their own, announced an energy and composed an array that his expression seemed to disavow, or at least to be indifferent to, and had the practical effect of toning down; as if he had been conscious that his nose, of the bravest, strongest curve and intrinsically a great success, was too bold and big for its social connections, that his mouth protested or at least asserted more than he cared to back it up to, that his chin and jaw were of too tactless an importance, and his fine eyes, above all, which suggested choice samples of the more or less precious stone called aquamarine, too disposed to darken with the force of a straight look—so that the right way to treat such an excess of resource had become for him quite the incongruous way, the cultivation of every sign and gage that liberties *might* be taken with him.

THE IVORY TOWER, Book 3, Chapter 1

Colonel Assingham

The Colonel sat back at his own ease, an ankle resting on the other knee and his eyes attentive to the good appearance of an extremely slender foot which he kept jerking in its neat integument of fine-spun black silk and patent leather. It seemed to confess, this member, to consciousness of military discipline, everything about it being as polished and perfect, as straight and tight and trim, as a soldier on parade. It went so far as to imply that some one or other would have "got" something or other, confinement to barracks or suppression of pay, if it hadn't been just as it was.

THE GOLDEN BOWL, Chapter 4

Charlotte Stant

What he accordingly saw for some seconds with intensity was a tall strong charming girl who wore for him at first exactly the air of her adventurous situation, a reference in all her person, in motion and gesture, in free vivid yet altogether happy indications of dress, from the becoming compactness of her hat to the shade of tan in her shoes, to winds and waves and customhouses, to far countries and long journeys, the knowledge of how and where and the habit, founded on experience, of not being afraid.

THE GOLDEN BOWL, Chapter 3

Chad Newsome (1)

Chad again fell back at this and, his hands pocketed, settled himself a little; in which posture he looked, though he rather anxiously smiled, only the more earnest. Then Strether seemed to see that he was really nervous, and he took that as what he would have called a wholesome sign. The only mark of it hitherto had been his more than once taking off and putting on his wide-brimmed crush hat. He had at this moment made the motion again to remove it, then had only pushed it back, so that it hung informally on his strong young grizzled crop. It was a touch that gave the note of the familiar—the intimate and the belated—to their quiet colloquy; and it was indeed by some such trivial aid that Strether became aware at the same moment of something else. He saw him in a flash as the young man marked out by women; and for a concentrated minute the dignity, the comparative austerity, as he funnily fancied it, of this character affected him almost with awe.

THE AMBASSADORS, Book 4, Chapter 1

Mrs. St. George

Mrs. St. George might have been the wife of a gentleman who "kept" books rather than wrote them, who carried on great affairs in the City and made better bargains than those that poets mostly make with publishers. Overt numbered her years at first as some thirty, and then ended by believing that she might approach her fiftieth. But she somehow in this case juggled away the excess and the difference—you only saw them in a rare glimpse, like the rabbit in the conjuror's sleeve. She was extraordinarily white, and her every element and item was pretty; her eyes, her ears, her hair, her voice, her hands, her feet—to which her relaxed attitude in her wicker chair gave a great publicity—and the numerous ribbons and trinkets with which she was bedecked. She looked as if she had put on her best clothes to go to church and then had decided they were too good for that and had stayed at home.

THE LESSON OF THE MASTER

Fannie Assingham

Type was there, at the worst, in Mrs. Assingham's dark neat head, on which the crisp black hair made waves so fine and so numerous that she looked even more in the fashion of the hour than she desired. Full of discriminations against the obvious, she had yet to accept a flagrant appearance and to make the best of misleading signs. Her richness of hue, her generous nose, her eyebrows marked like those of an actress—these things, with an added amplitude of person on which middle age had set its seal, seemed to present her insistently as a daughter of the South, or still more of the East, a creature formed by hammocks and divans, fed upon sherbets and waited upon by slaves. She looked as if her most active effort might be to take up, as she lay back, her mandolin, or to share a sugared fruit with a pet gazelle. She was in fact however neither a pampered Jewess nor a lazy Creole; New York had been recordedly her birthplace and "Europe" punctually her discipline.

THE GOLDEN BOWL, Chapter 2

Mamie Newsome

She was robust and conveniently tall; just a trifle too bloodlessly fair perhaps, but with a pleasant public familiar radiance that affirmed her vitality. She might have been "receiving" for Woollett, wherever she found herself, and there was something in her manner, her tone, her motion, her pretty blue eyes, her pretty perfect teeth and her very small, too small, nose, that immediately placed her, to the fancy, between the windows of a hot bright room in which voices were high— up at that end to which people were brought to be "presented." What Mamie was like was the happy bride, the bride after the church and just before going away.

THE AMBASSADORS, Book 8, Chapter 2

Mrs. Tristram

It was since she had come to live in Europe that she had begun to take the matter philosophically. Her observation, accurately exercised here, had suggested to her that a woman's social service resides not in what she is but in what she appears, and that in the labyrinth of appearances she may always make others lose their clue if she only keeps her own. She had encountered so many women who pleased without beauty that she began to believe she had discovered her refuge. She had once heard an enthusiastic musician, out of patience with a gifted bungler, declare that a fine voice is really an obstacle to singing properly; and it occurred to her that it might perhaps be equally true that a beautiful face is an obstacle to the acquisition of charming manners. Mrs. Tristram then undertook to persuade by grace, and she brought to the task no small ingenuity.

THE AMERICAN, Chapter 3

Mr. Brookenham

He had a pale cold face, marked and made regular, made even in a manner handsome, by a hardness of line in which, oddly, there was no significance, no accent. Clean-shaven, slightly bald, with unlighted grey eyes and a mouth that gave the impression of not working easily, he suggested a stippled drawing by an inferior master. Lean moreover and stiff, and with the air of having here and there in his person a bone or two more than his share, he had once or twice, at fancy-balls, been thought striking in a dress copied from one of Holbein's English portraits.

THE AWKWARD AGE, Book 2, Chapter 3

Gloriani

This assault of images became for a moment, in the address of the distinguished sculptor, almost formidable: Gloriani showed him, in such perfect confidence, on Chad's introduction of him, a fine worn handsome face, a face that was like an open letter in a foreign tongue. With his genius in his eyes, his manners on his lips, his long career behind him and his honours and rewards all round, the great artist, in the course of a single sustained look and a few words of delight at receiving him, affected our friend as a dazzling prodigy of type.

THE AMBASSADORS, Book 5, Chapter 1

Maggie, the Princess (1)

She stood there before him with that particular suggestion in her aspect to which even the long habit of their life together hadn't closed his sense—the appearance of some slight slim draped "antique" of Vatican or Capitoline halls, late and refined, rare as a note and immortal as a link, set in motion by the miraculous infusion of a modern impulse and yet, for all the sudden freedom of folds and footsteps forsaken after centuries by their pedestal, keeping still the quality, the perfect felicity, of the statue; the blurred absent eyes, the smoothed elegant nameless head, the impersonal flit of a creature lost in an alien age and passing as an image in worn relief round and round a precious vase.

THE GOLDEN BOWL, Chapter 10

Maggie, the Princess (2)

It had ever been her sign that she was for all occasions *found* ready, without loose ends or exposed accessories or unremoved superfluities; a suggestion of the swept and garnished, in her whole splendid yet thereby more or less encumbered and embroidered setting, that re flected her small still passion for order and symmetry, for objects with their backs to the walls, and spoke even of some probable reference in her American blood to dusting and polishing New England grandmothers. If her apartment was "princely," in the clearness of the lingering day, she looked as if she had been carried there prepared, all attired and decorated, like some holy image in a procession, and left precisely to show what wonder she could work under pressure.

THE GOLDEN BOWL, Chapter 32

The Priest as Luncheon Guest

She met the good priest's eyes before they separated, and priests were really at the worst, so to speak, such wonderful people that she believed him for an instant on the verge of saying to her in abysmal softness: "Go to Mrs. Verver, my child—*you* go: you'll find you can help her." This didn't come, however; nothing came but the renewed twiddle of thumbs over the satisfied stomach and the full flush, the comical candour, of reference to the hand employed at Fawns for mayonnaise of salmon.

THE GOLDEN BOWL, Chapter 39

Lord John

This younger son of a noble matron recognised even by himself as terrible enjoyed in no immediate or aggressive manner any imputable private heritage or privilege of arrogance. He would on the contrary have irradiated fineness if his lustre hadn't been a little prematurely dimmed. Active yet insubstantial, he was slight and short and a trifle too punctually, though not yet quite lamentably, bald. Delicacy was in the arch of his eyebrow, the finish of his facial line, the economy of "treatment" by which his negative nose had been enabled to look important and his meagre mouth to smile its spareness away. He had pleasant but hard little eyes—they glittered, handsomely, without promise—and a neatness, a coolness and an ease, a clear instinct for making point take, on his behalf, the place of weight and immunity that of capacity, which represented somehow the art of living at a high pitch and yet at a low cost. There was that in his satisfied air which still suggested sharp wants.

> THE OUTCRY, Book 1, Chapter 1

Abel Gaw

"Don't you get tired," she put to him, "of just sitting round here?"

He turned to her his small neat finely-wrinkled face, of an extreme yellowish pallor and which somehow suggested at this end of time an empty glass that had yet held for years so much strong wine that a faint golden tinge still lingered on from it. "I can't get any more tired than I am already."

> THE IVORY TOWER, Book 1, Chapter 1

Mrs. Medwin

This lady was not in the first flush of her youth; her appearance—the scattered remains of beauty manipulated by taste—resembled one of the light repasts in which the fragments of yesterday's dinner figure with a conscious ease that makes up for the want of presence. She was perhaps of an effect still too immediate to be called interesting, but she was candid, gentle and surprised—not fatiguingly surprised, only just in the right degree; and her white face—it was too white—with the fixed eyes, the somewhat touzled hair and the Louis Seize hat, might at the end of the very long neck have suggested the head of a princess carried, in a revolution, on a pike.

MRS. MEDWIN

Waymarsh

He had a large handsome head and a large sallow seamed face—a striking significant physiognomic total, the upper range of which, the great political brow, the thick loose hair, the dark fuliginous eyes, recalled even to a generation whose standard had dreadfully deviated the impressive image, familiar by engravings and busts, of some great national worthy of the earlier part of the mid-century. The legend had been in later years that as the lower part of his face, which was weak, and slightly crooked, spoiled the likeness, this was the real reason for the growth of his beard, which might have seemed to spoil it for those not in the secret. He shook his mane; he fixed, with his admirable eyes, his auditor or his observer; he met you as if you had knocked and he had bidden you enter.

THE AMBASSADORS, Book 1, Chapter 2

Mr. Perriam

Mr. Perriam was short and massive—Mrs. Wix remarked afterwards that he was "too fat for the pace"; and it would have been difficult to say of him whether his head were more bald or his black moustache more bushy. He seemed also to have moustaches over his eyes, which, however, by no means prevented these polished little globes from rolling round the room as if they had been billiard-balls impelled by Ida's celebrated stroke. Mr. Perriam wore on the hand that pulled his moustache a diamond of dazzling lustre, in consequence of which and of his general weight and mystery our young lady observed on his departure that if he had only had a turban he would have been quite her idea of a heathen Turk.

"He's quite my idea," Mrs. Wix replied, "of a heathen Jew."

WHAT MAISIE KNEW, Chapter 11

Ethel Stormer

She gave one to understand she meant to do all she could for herself. She was long-necked and near-sighted and striking, and I thought I had never seen sweet seventeen in a form so hard and high and dry. She was cold and affected and ambitious, and she carried an eyeglass with a long handle, which she put up whenever she wanted not to see. She had come out, as the phrase is, immensely; and yet I felt as if she were surrounded with a spiked iron railing. What she meant to do for herself was to marry, and it was the only thing, I think that she meant to do for any one else; yet who would be inspired to clamber over that bristling barrier?

GREVILLE FANE

"Aunt Maud" Lowder

She would have been meanwhile a wonderful lioness for a show, an extraordinary figure in a cage or anywhere; majestic, magnificent, high-coloured, all brilliant gloss, perpetual satin, twinkling bugles and flashing gems, with a lustre of agate eyes, a sheen of raven hair, a polish of complexion that was like that of well-kept china and that—as if the skin were too tight—told especially at curves and corners. Her niece had a quiet name for her—Britannia of the Market Place, with a pen in her ear.

THE WINGS OF THE DOVE, Chapter 2

Miss Birdseye

She had a sad, soft, pale face, which (and it was the effect of her whole head) looked as if it had been soaked, blurred, and made vague by exposure to some slow dissolvent. The long practice of philanthropy had not given accent to her features; it had rubbed out their transitions, their meanings. The waves of sympathy, of enthusiasm, had wrought upon them in the same way in which the waves of time finally modify the surface of old marble busts, gradually washing away their sharpness, their details. In her large countenance her dim little smile scarcely showed. It was a mere sketch of a smile, a kind of instalment, or payment on account; it seemed to say that she would smile more if she had time, but that you could see, without this, that she was gentle and easy to beguile.

THE BOSTONIANS, Chapter 4

The American Scene

The Capitol, Washington, D.C.

The encounter was happy on both sides, and he accompanied them through the queer and endless interior, through labyrinths of bleak bare development, into legislative and judicial halls. He thought it a hideous place; he had seen it all before and asked himself what senseless game he was playing. In the lower House were certain bedaubed walls, in the basest style of imitation, which made him feel faintly sick, not to speak of a lobby adorned with artless prints and photographs of eminent defunct Congressmen that was all too serious for a joke and too comic for a Valhalla. But Pandora was greatly interested; she thought the Capitol very fine; it was easy to criticise the details, but as a whole it was the most impressive building she had ever seen.

PANDORA

Mount Vernon

Association does, at Mount Vernon, simply what it likes with us—it is of so beautiful and noble a sort; and to this end it begins by making us unfit to say whether or no we would in its absence have noticed the house for any material grace at all. We scarce care more for its being proved picturesque, the house, than for its being proved plain; its architectural interest and architectural nullity become one and the same thing for us. If asked what we should think of it if it hadn't been, or if we hadn't known it for, Washington's, we retort that the inquiry is inane, since it is not the possessive case, but the straight, serene nominative, that we are dealing with. The whole thing *is* Washington.

THE AMERICAN SCENE, Chapter 11

Senators

The legislative session was over, but this made little difference in the aspect of Mrs. Bonnycastle's rooms, which even at the height of the congressional season could scarce be said to overflow with the representatives of the people. They were garnished with an occasional Senator, whose movements and utterances often appeared to be regarded with a mixture of alarm and indulgence, as if they would be disappointing if they weren't rather odd and yet might be dangerous if not carefully watched. Our young man had come to entertain a kindness for these conscript fathers of invisible families, who had something of the toga in the voluminous folds of their conversation, but were otherwise rather bare and bald, with stony wrinkles in their faces, like busts and statues of ancient law-givers. There seemed to him something chill and exposed in their being at once so exalted and so naked; there were frequent lonesome glances in their eyes, as if in the social world their legislative consciousness longed for the warmth of a few comfortable laws ready-made.

PANDORA

Mrs. Bonnycastle (Mrs. Henry Adams) as Hostess

Toward the end of the social year, in those soft scented days of the Washington spring when the air began to show a southern glow and the Squares and Circles (to which the wide empty avenues converged according to a plan so ingenious, yet so bewildering) to flush with pink blossom and to make one wish to sit on benches—

under this magic of expansion and condonation Mrs. Bonnycastle, who during the winter had been a good deal on the defensive, relaxed her vigilance a little, became whimsically wilful, vernally reckless, as it were, and ceased to calculate the consequences of an hospitality which a reference to the back files or even to the morning's issue of the newspapers might easily prove a mistake.

PANDORA

The New England Village

These communities stray so little from the type, that you often ask yourself by what sign or difference you know one from the other. The goodly elms, on either side of the large straight "street," rise from their grassy margin in double, ever and anon in triple, file; the white paint, on wooden walls, amid open dooryards, reaffirms itself eternally behind them—though handing back, during the best of the season, with a sun-checkered, "amusing" vagueness; while the great verdurous vista, the high canopy of meeting branches, has the air of consciously playing the trick and carrying off the picture.

THE AMERICAN SCENE, Chapter 1

Secrets behind the New England Village Facades

But the strangest link in the chain, and quite the horridest, was this other, of high value to the restless analyst—that, as the "interesting" puts in its note but where it can and where it will, so the village street and the lonely farm and the hillside cabin became positively richer objects under the smutch of imputation; twitched with a grim effect the thinness of their mantle, shook out of its folds such crudity and levity as they might, and borrowed, for dignity, a shade of the darkness of Cenci drama, of monstrous legend, of old Greek tragedy, and thus helped themselves out for the story-seeker more patient almost of anything than of flatness.

THE AMERICAN SCENE, Chapter 1

Concord River

I hung over Concord River then as long as I could, and recalled how Thoreau, Hawthorne, Emerson himself, have expressed with due sympathy the sense of this full, slow, sleepy, meadowy flood, which sets its pace and takes its twists like some large obese benevolent person, scarce so frankly unsociable as to pass you at all. It had watched the Fight, it even now confesses, without a quickening of its current, and it draws along the woods and the orchards and the fields with the purr of a mild domesticated cat who rubs against the family and the furniture.

THE AMERICAN SCENE, Chapter 8

Mr. and Mrs. Rimmle

The head of the family was the widow of a great public character whose speeches on anniversaries formed a part of the body of national eloquence spouted in the New England schools by little boys covetous of the most marked, though perhaps the easiest, distinction. He was reported to have been celebrated and in such fine declamatory connections that he seemed to gesticulate even from the tomb.

EUROPE

Boston and the Charles River

The western windows of Olive's dressing-room, looking over the water, took in the red sunsets of winter; the long, low bridge that crawled, on its staggering posts, across the Charles; the casual patches of ice and snow; the desolate suburban horizons, peeled and made bald by the rigour of the season; the general hard, cold void of the prospect; the extrusion, at Charlestown, at Cambridge, of a few chimneys and steeples, straight, sordid tubes of factories and engine-shops, or spare, heavenward finger of the New England meeting-house. Verena thought such a view lovely, and she was by no means without excuse when, as the afternoon closed, the ugly picture was tinted with a clear, cold rosiness. The air, in its windless chill, seemed to tinkle like a crystal, the faintest gradations of tone were perceptible in the sky, the west became deep and delicate, everything grew doubly distinct before taking on the dimness of evening. These agreeable effects used to light up that end of the drawing-room, and Olive often sat at the window with her companion before it was time for the lamp.

THE BOSTONIANS, Chapter 20

Harvard Memorial Hall

It stands there for duty and honour, it speaks of sacrifice and example, seems a kind of temple to youth, manhood, generosity. Most of them were young, all were in their prime, and all of them had fallen; this simple idea hovers before the visitor and makes him read with tenderness each name and place-name, often without other history, and forgotten Southern battles. For Ransom these things were not a challenge nor a taunt; they touched him with respect, with the sentiment of beauty. He was capable of being a generous foeman, and he forgot, now, the whole question of sides and parties; the simple emotion of the old fighting-time came back to him, and the monument around him seemed an embodiment of that memory; it arched over friends as well as enemies, the victims of defeat as well as the sons of triumph.

THE BOSTONIANS, Chapter 20

The Museum in Richmond

The sorry objects about were old Confederate documents, already sallow with time, framed letters, orders, autographs, extracts, tatters of a paper-currency in the last stages of vitiation; together with faded portraits of faded worthies, primitive products of the camera, the crayon, the brush; of all of which she did the honours with a gentle florid reverence that opened wide, for the musing visitor, as he lingered and strolled, the portals, as it were, of a singularly interesting "case." It was the case of the beautiful, the attaching oddity of the general Southern state of mind, or stage of feeling, in relation to that heritage of woe and of glory of which the mementos surrounded me.

THE AMERICAN SCENE, Chapter 112

The Lesson of Richmond

What was I tasting of, at that time of day, and with intensity, but the far consequences of things, made absolutely majestic by their weight and duration? I was tasting, mystically, of the very essence of the old Southern idea—the hugest fallacy, as it hovered there to one's backward, one's ranging vision, for which hundreds of thousands of men had ever laid down their lives. I was tasting of the very bitterness of the immense, grotesque, defeated project—the project, extravagant, fantastic, and to-day pathetic in its folly, of a vast Slave State (as the old term ran) artfully, savingly isolated in the world that was to contain it and trade with it. This was what everything round me meant—that that absurdity had once flourished there.

THE AMERICAN SCENE, Chapter 12

George W. Vanderbilt's "Biltmore" (1)

I had, by a deviation, spent a week in a castle of enchantment; but if this modern miracle, of which the mountains of North Carolina happened to be the scene, would have been almost anywhere miraculous, I could at least take it as testifying, all relevantly, all directly, for the presence, as distinguished from the absence, of feature. One felt how, in this light, the extent and the splendor of such a place was but a detail; these things were accidents without which the great effect, the element that, in the beautiful empty air, made all the difference, would still have prevailed. What was this element but just the affirmation of resources?—made with great emphasis indeed, but in a clear and exemplary way; so that if large wealth represented some of them, an idea, a fine cluster of ideas, a will, a purpose, a patience, an intelligence, a store of knowledge, immediately workable things, represented the others.

THE AMERICAN SCENE, Chapter 13

George W. Vanderbilt's "Biltmore" (2)

Roll three or four Rothschild houses into one, surround them with a principality of mountain, lake and forest, 200,000 acres, surround *that* with vast states of niggery desolation and make it impossible, through distance and time, to get anyone to stay with you, and you have the bloated Biltmore . . . utterly unaddressed to any possible arrangement of life or state of society.

Letter, 1905

The American City

The collective consciousness, in however empty an air, gasps for a relation, as intimate as possible, to something superior, something as central as possible, from which it may more or less have proceeded and round which its life may revolve—and its dim desire is always, I think, to do it justice, that this object or presence shall have had as much as possible an heroic or romantic association. But the difficulty is that in these later times, among such aggregations, the heroic and romantic elements, even under the earliest rude stress, have been all too tragically obscure, belonged to smothered, unwritten, almost unconscious private history: so that the central something, the social *point de repère*, has had to be extemporized rather pitifully after the fact, and made to consist of the biggest hotel or the biggest common school, the biggest factory, the biggest newspaper office, or, for climax of desperation, the house of the biggest millionaire.

THE AMERICAN SCENE, Chapter 9

Hawthorne's America

No State, in the European sense of the word, and indeed barely a specific national name. No sovereign, no court, no personal loyalty, no aristocracy, no church, no clergy, no army, no diplomatic service, no country gentlemen, no palaces, no castles, nor manors, nor old country-houses, nor parsonages, nor thatched cottages, nor ivied ruins; no cathedrals, nor abbeys, nor little Norman churches, nor great universities, nor public schools—no Oxford, nor Eton, nor Harrow; no literature, no novels, no museums, no pictures, no political society, no sporting class—nor Epsom nor Ascot!

HAWTHORNE, Chapter 2

The American Heiress

A less vulgarly, less obviously purchasing or parading person she couldn't have imagined; but it was, all the same, the truth of truths that the girl couldn't get away from her wealth. She might leave her conscientious companion as freely alone with it as possible and never ask a question, scarce even tolerate a reference; but it was in the fine folds of the helplessly expensive little black frock; it was in the curious and splendid coils of hair, "done" with no eye whatever to the *mode du jour*; it lurked between the leaves of the uncut but antiquted Tauchnitz volume. She couldn't dress it away, nor walk it away, nor read it away, nor think it away; she could neither smile it away in any dreamy absence nor blow it away in any softened sigh. She couldn't have lost it if she had tried—that was what it was to be really rich. It had to be the thing you were.

THE WINGS OF THE DOVE, Chapter 5

Making Money

What prevails, what sets the tune, is the American scale of gain, more magnificent than any other, and the fact that the whole assumption, the whole theory of life, is that of the individual's participation in it, that of his being more or less punctually and more or less effectually "squared." To make so much money that you won't, that you don't "mind," don't mind anything—that is absolutely, I think, the main American formula. Thus your making no money—or so little that it passes there for none—and being thereby distinctly reduced to minding, amounts to your being reduced to the knowledge that America is no place for you.

THE AMERICAN SCENE, Chapter 7

The Newspaper Column

The young lady, frankly, a graceful amateur journalist, had made use of her gathered material; she had addressed to a newspaper in her native city a letter as long, as confidential, as "chatty," as full of headlong history and limping legend, of aberration and confusion, as she might have indited to the most trusted of friends. The friend trusted had been, as happened, simply the biggest "reading public" in the world, and the performance, typographically bristling, had winged its way back to its dishonoured nest like some monstrous black bird or beetle, an embodiment of popping eyes, a whirl of brandished feathers and claws.

Preface to THE REVERBERATOR

Personalities

The James Family and Religion

Well do I remember, nonetheless, how I was troubled all along just by this particular crookedness of our being so extremely religious without having, as it were, anything in the least classified or striking to show for it; so that the measure of other-worldliness pervading our premises was rather a waste, though at the same time oddly enough a congestion—projecting outwardly as it did no single one of those usual symptoms of propriety any of which, gathered at a venture from the general prospect, might by my sense have served: I shouldn't have been particular, I thought, as to the selection.

NOTES OF A SON AND BROTHER, Chapter 6

The Senior Henry James's Answer to the Question Of Religion

"What church do you go to?"—the challenge took in childish circles that searching form. To which I must add as well that our "fending" in this fashion for ourselves didn't so prepare us for invidious remark—remark I mean upon our pewless state, which involved, in my imagination, much the same discredit that a houseless or a cookless would have done—as to hush in my breast the appeal to our parents, not for religious instruction (of which we had plenty, and of the most charming and familiar) but simply for instruction (a very different thing) as to where we should say we "went," in our world, under cold scrutiny or derisive comment. It was colder than any criticism, I recall, to hear our father reply that we could plead nothing less than the whole privilege of Christendom.

A SMALL BOY AND OTHERS, Chapter 17

Henry James Sr. (1)

It was in no world of close application that our wondrous parent moved, and his indifference at the first blush to the manifestation of special and marketable talents and faculties, restlessly outward purposes of whatever would-be "successful" sort, was apt to be surpassable only by his delight subsequently taken in our attested and visible results, the very fruits of application; as to which the possibility, perhaps even the virtual guarantee, hadn't so much left him cold in advance as made him adversely and "spiritually" hot. The sense of that word was the most living thing in the world for him—to the point that the spiritual simply meant to him the practical and the successful, so far as he could get into touch with such denominations, or so far, that is, as he could face them or care for them *a priori*.

> NOTES OF A SON AND BROTHER, Chapter 3

Henry James Sr. (2)

Strong is my conviction that our mystery, in the event, yielded almost at once to our elation, for no tradition had a brighter household life with us than that of our father's headlong impatience. He moved in a cloud, if not rather in a high radiance, of precipitation and divulgation, a chartered rebel against cold reserves. The good news in his hand refused under any persuasion to grow stale, the sense of communicable pleasure in his breast was positively explosive; so that we saw those "surprises" in which he had conspired with our mother for our benefit converted by him in every case, under our shamelessly encouraged guesses, into common conspiracies against her—against her knowing, that is, how thoroughly we were all compromised.

> A SMALL BOY AND OTHERS, Chapter 7

The Harvard Law Professor

Of the third of our instructors I mainly recall that he represented dryness and hardness, prose unrelieved, at their deadliest—partly perhaps because he was most master of his subject. He was none the less placeable for these things withal, and what mainly comes back to me of him is the full sufficiency with which he made me ask myself how I *could* for a moment have seen myself really browse in any field where the marks of the shepherd were such an oblong dome of a bare cranium, such a fringe of dropping little ringlets toward its base, and a mouth so meanly retentive, so ignorant of style, as I made out, above a chin so indifferent to the duty, or at least to the opportunity, of chins.

NOTES OF A SON AND BROTHER, Chapter 10

Alfred Tennyson and Mrs. Charles Greville

He must have been of the party, and Mrs. Greville quite independently must, since I catch again the vision of her, so expansively and voluminously seated that she might fairly have been couchant, so to say, for the proposed characteristic act—there was a deliberation about it that precluded the idea of a spring; that, namely, of addressing something of the Laureate's very own to the Laureate's very face. He took these things with a gruff philosophy—and could always repay them, on the spot, in heavily-shovelled coin of the same mint.

THE MIDDLE YEARS, Chapter 6

Minnie Temple

She was really to remain, for our appreciation, the supreme case of a taste for life as life, as personal living; of an endlessly active and yet somehow a careless, an illusionless, a sublimely forewarned curiosity about it: something that made her, slim and fair and quick, all straightness and charming tossed head, with long light and yet almost sliding steps and a large light postponing, renouncing laugh, the very muse or amateur priestess of rash speculation.

NOTES OF A SON AND BROTHER, Chapter 4

George Eliot

I see again our bland, benign, commiserating hostess beside the fire in a chill desert of a room where the master of the house guarded the opposite hearthstone, and I catch once more the impression of no occurrence of anything at all appreciable but their liking us to have come, with our terribly trivial contribution, mainly from a prevision of how they should more devoutly like it when we departed.

THE MIDDLE YEARS, Chapter 5

G. H. Lewes

I returned to the doorstep, whence I still see him reissue from the room we had just left and hurry toward me across the hall shaking high the pair of blue-bound volumes his allusion to the uninvited, the verily importunate loan of which by Mrs. Greville had lingered on the air after his dash in quest of them: "Ah those books—take them away, please, away, away!" I hear him unreservedly plead while he thrusts them again at me, and I scurry back into our conveyance, where, and where only, settled afresh with my companion, I venture to assure myself of the horrid truth that had squinted at me as I relieved our good friend of his superfluity. What indeed was this superfluity but the two volumes of my own precious "last"?

THE MIDDLE YEARS, Chapter 5

An Aging Actress

She struck me as the very image of mere sore histrionic habit and use, a worn and weary, a battered even though almost sordidly smoothed, *thing* of the theatre, very much as an old infinitely-handled and greasy violoncello of the orchestra might have been. It was but an effect doubtless of the heat that she scarcely seemed clad at all; slippered, shuffling and, though somehow hatted and vaguely veiled or streamered, wrapt in a gauzy sketch of a dressing-gown, she pointed to my extravagant attention the moral of thankless personal service, of the reverse of the picture, of the cost of "amusing the public" in a case of amusing it, as who should say, every hour.

A SMALL BOY AND OTHERS, Chapter 11

W. E. Gladstone

The sublime old man was in the drawing room last night after dinner and talked about bookbinding and the vulgarity of the son of a Tory Duke having talked about "pooh-poohing" something or other in the House of Commons: a vile new verb, unworthy of that high assembly. Today he lunched downstairs and discoursed about the new version of the Scriptures and the advisability of having at Oxford both a lay and a clerical professor of Hebrew.

Letter to Lord Rosebery, 1884

Gladstone's mind doesn't interest me much: it appears to have no preferences, to care equally for all subjects—which is tiresome.

Letter to William James, 1884

W. M. Thackeray

It was but a short time before those days that the great Mr. Thackeray had come to America to lecture on The English Humourists, and still present to me is the voice proceeding from my father's library, in which some glimpse of me hovering, at an opening of the door, in passage or on staircase, prompted him to the formidable words: "Come here, little boy, and show me your extraordinary jacket!" My sense of my jacket became from that hour a heavy one—further enriched as my vision is by my shyness of posture before the seated, the celebrated visitor, who struck me, in the sunny light of the animated room, as enormously big and who, though he laid on my shoulder the hand of benevolence, bent on my native costume the spectacles of wonder.

A SMALL BOY AND OTHERS, Chapter 7

R. W. Emerson (1)

I "visualise" at any rate the winter firelight of our back-parlour at dusk and the great Emerson—I knew he was great, greater than any of our friends—sitting in it between my parents, before the lamps had been lighted, as a visitor consentingly housed only could have done, and affecting me the more as an apparition sinuously and, I held, elegantly slim, benevolently aquiline, and commanding a tone alien, beautifully alien, to any we heard roundabout, that he bent this benignity upon me by an invitation to draw nearer to him, off the hearth-rug, and know myself as never yet, as I was not indeed to know myself again for years, in touch with the wonder of Boston.

NOTES OF A SON AND BROTHER, Chapter 7

Emerson (2)

We have the impression, somehow, that life had never bribed him to look at anything but the soul; and indeed in the world in which he grew up and lived the bribes and lures, the beguilements and prizes, were few. He was in an admirable position for showing, what he constantly endeavoured to show, that the prize was within. . . . I well remember my impression of this on walking with him in the autumn of 1872 through the galleries of the Louvre and, later that winter, through those of the Vatican: his perception of the objects contained in these collections was of the most general order. I was struck with the anomaly of a man so refined and intelligent being so little spoken to by works of art. It would be more exact to say that certain chords were wholly absent; the tune was played, the tune of life and literature, altogether on those that remained.

PARTIAL PORTRAITS

Anthony Trollope

It was once the fortune of the author of these lines to cross the Atlantic in his company, and he has never forgotten the magnificent example of plain persistence that it was in the power of the eminent novelist to give on that occasion. The season was unpropitious, the vessel overcrowded, the voyage detestable; but Trollope shut himself up in his cabin every morning for a purpose which, on the part of a distinguished writer who was also an invulnerable sailor, could only be communion with the muse. He drove his pen as steadily on the tumbling ocean as in Montague Square; and as his voyages were many, it was his practice before sailing to come down to the ship and confer with the carpenter, who was instructed to rig up a rough writing-table in his small sea-chamber. Trollope has been accused of being deficient in imagination, but in the face of such a fact as that the charge will scarcely seem just. The power to shut one's eyes, one's ears (to say nothing of another sense), upon the scenery of a pitching Cunarder and open them upon the loves and sorrows of Lily Dale or the conjugal embarrassments of Lady Glencora Palliser, is certainly a faculty which could take to itself wings.

PARTIAL PORTRAITS

Henry Adams and John La Farge

Many thanks for your sympathetic words about Adams. I like him, but suffer from his monotonous disappointed pessimism. Besides, he is what I should have liked to be—a man of wealth and leisure, able to satisfy all his curiosities, while I am a penniless toiler—so what can *I* do for him? However, when the poor dear is in London I don't fail to do what I can. I don't know where he is now. He kindly forsakes the fleshpots of the Bristol for the very dry casseroles of my lofty-lowly garret. I wish you could have had at Tillypronie his and my very old friend (and his late travelling companion) John La Farge, one of the most extraordinary and agreeable of men, a remarkable combination of France and America, who spent the other day with me in London on his way back to New York, causing me to wonder afresh at his combination of social and artistic endowments and yet how Adams and he could either of them have failed to murder the other in Polynesia. Fortunately each lives to prove the other's self-control.

Letter to Sir John Clark, 1891

Vernon Lee

The most intelligent person in Florence is Violet Paget [Vernon Lee] who has lived there all her life, and receives every day, from 4 to 7, and as often in the evening as people will come to her. She is exceedingly ugly, not "well off," disputatious, contradictious and perverse, has a clever, paralysed half-brother, Edward Hamilton, formerly in diplomacy—who is always in her salon, bedridden or rather sofa-ridden—and also a grotesque, deformed, invalidical, *posing* little old mother, and a father in the highest degree unpleasant, mysterious and sinister, who walks *all day*, all over Florence, hates his stepson, and hasn't sat down to table with his family for twenty years. Yet in spite of these drawbacks, Miss Paget's intellectual and social energy are so great, that she attracts all the world to her drawing room, discusses all things in *any* language, and understands some, drives her pen, glares through her spectacles and keeps up her courage. She has a *mind*—almost the only one in Florence.

Letter to Grace Norton, 1887

Portraits of Places

Rome

He grew intimately, passionately fond of all Roman sights and sensations. He could not have defined nor explained the nature of his relish, nor have made up the sum of it by adding together his calculable pleasures. It was a large, vague, idle, half-profitless emotion, of which perhaps the most pertinent thing that might be said was that it brought with it a relaxed acceptance of the present, the actual, the sensuous—of existence on the terms of the moment. Whether it be that one tacitly concedes to the Roman Church the monopoly of a guarantee of immortality, so that if one is indisposed to bargain with her for the precious gift one must do without it altogether; or whether in an atmosphere so heavily weighted with echoes and memories one grows to believe that there is nothing in one's consciousness not predetermined to moulder and crumble and become dust for the feet and possible malaria for the lungs of future generations—the fact at least remains that one parts half willingly with one's hopes in Rome.

RODERICK HUDSON, Chapter 9

Rome and Daisy Miller

A few days after his brief interview with her mother he came across her at that supreme seat of flowering desolation known as the Palace of the Caesars. The early Roman spring had filled the air with bloom and perfume, and the rugged surface of the Palatine was muffled with tender verdure. Daisy moved at her ease over the great mounds of ruin that are embanked with mossy marble and paved with monumental inscriptions. It seemed to him he had never known Rome so lovely as just then. He looked off at the enchanting harmony of line and colour that remotely encircles the city—he inhaled the softly humid odours and felt the freshness of the year and the antiquity of the place re-affirm themselves in deep interfusion. It struck him also that Daisy had never showed to the eye for so utterly charming; but this had been his conviction on every occasion of their meeting.

DAISY MILLER, Chapter 4

The Osmonds' Palace

The object of Mr. Rosier's well-regulated affection dwelt in a high house in the very heart of Rome; a dark and massive structure overlooking a sunny *piazzetta* in the neighbourhood of the Farnese Palace. In a palace, too, little Pansy lived—a palace by Roman measure, but a dungeon to poor Rosier's apprehensive mind. It seemed to him of evil omen that the young lady he wished to marry, and whose fastidious father he doubted of his ability to conciliate, should be immured in a kind of domestic fortress, a pile which bore a stern old Roman name, which smelt of historic deeds, of crime and craft and violence, which was mentioned in "Murray" and visited by tourists who looked, on a vague survey, disappointed and depressed, and which had frescoes by Caravaggio in the *piano nobile* and a row of mutilated statues and dusty urns in the wide, nobly-arched loggia overhanging the damp court where a fountain gushed out of a mossy niche.

THE PORTRAIT OF A LADY, Chapter 36

Venice (1)

It was a Venice all of evil that had broken out for them alike, so that they were together in their anxiety, if they really could have met on it; a Venice of cold, lashing rain from a low black sky, of wicked wind raging through narrow passes, of general arrest and interruption, with the people engaged in all the water-life huddled, stranded and wageless, bored and cynical, under archways and bridges.

THE WINGS OF THE DOVE, Chapter 30

Venice (2)

Venice glowed and plashed and called and chimed again; the air was like a clap of hands, and the scattered pinks, yellows, blues, sea-greens, were like a hanging-out of vivid stuffs, a laying down of fine carpets.

THE WINGS OF THE DOVE, Chapter 32

The Venetian Palazzo

Not yet so much as this morning had she felt herself sink into possession; gratefully glad that the warmth of the southern summer was still in the high, florid rooms, palatial chambers where hard, cool pavements took reflections in their lifelong polish, and where the sun on the stirred sea-water, flickering up through open windows, plyed over the painted "subjects" in the splendid ceilings—medallions of purple and brown, of brave old melancholy colour, medals as of old reddened gold, embossed and beribboned, all toned with time and all flourished and scolloped and gilded about, set in their great moulded and figured concavity (a nest of white cherubs, friendly creatures of the air).

THE WINGS OF THE DOVE, Chapter 24

Paris

His greatest uneasiness seemed to peep at him out of the imminent impression that almost any acceptance of Paris might give one's authority away. It hung before him this morning, the vast bright Babylon, like some huge iridescent object, a jewel brilliant and hard, in which parts were not to be discriminated nor differences comfortably marked. It twinkled and trembled and melted together, and what seemed all surface one moment seemed all depth the next.

THE AMBASSADORS, Book 2, Chapter 2

Gloriani's Hôtel (the Musée Rodin)

The place itself was a great impression—a small pavilion, clear faced and sequestered, an effect of polished parquet, of fine white panel and spare sallow gilt, of decoration delicate and rare, in the heart of the Faubourg Saint-Germain and on the edge of a cluster of gardens attached to old noble houses. Far back from streets and unsuspected by crowds, reached by a long passage and a quiet court, it was as striking to the unprepared mind, he immediately saw, as a treasure dug up; giving him too, more than anything yet, the note of the range of the immeasureable town and sweeping away, as by a last brave brush, his usual landmarks and terms.

THE AMBASSADORS, Book 5, Chapter 1

The Different Forms of "Style" in the Louvre

To distinguish among these, in the charged and colored and confounding air, was difficult—it discouraged and defied; which was doubtless why my impression originally best entertained was that of those magnificent parts of the great gallery simply not inviting us to distinguish. They only arched over us in the wonder of their endless golden riot and relief, figured and flourished in perpetual revolution, breaking into great high-hung circles and symmetries of squandered picture, opening into deep outward embrasures that threw off the rest of monumental Paris somehow as a told story, a sort of wrought effect or bold ambiguity for a vista, and yet held it there, at every point, as a vast bright gage, even at moments a felt adventure, of experience.

A SMALL BOY AND OTHERS, Chapter 25

A "Hôtel" in the Old Faubourg

The light in her beautiful formal room was dim, though it would do, as everything would always do; the hot night had kept out lamps, but there was a pair of clusters of candles that glimmered over the chimney-piece like the tall tapers of an altar. The windows were all open, their redundant hangings swaying a little, and he heard once more, from the empty court, the small plash of the fountain. From beyond this, and as from a great distance came, as if excited and exciting, the vague voice of Paris. Strether had all along been subject to sudden gusts of fancy in connexion with such matters as these—odd starts of the historic sense, suppositions and divinations with no warrant but their intensity. Thus and so, on the eve of the great recorded dates, the days and nights of revolution, the sounds had come in, the omens, the beginnings broken out. They were the smell of revolution, the smell of the public temper—or perhaps simply the smell of blood.

THE AMBASSADORS, Book 12, Chapter 1

The Garden of the Tuileries

In the garden of the Tuileries he had lingered, on two or three spots, to look; it was as if the wonderful Paris spring had stayed him as he roamed. The prompt Paris morning struck its cheerful notes—in a soft breeze and a sprinkled smell, in the light flit, over the garden-floor, of bareheaded girls with the buckled strap of oblong boxes, in the type of ancient thrifty persons basking betimes where terrace-walls were warm, in the blue-frocked brass-labelled officialism of humble rakers and scrapers, in the deep references of a straight-pacing priest or the sharp ones of a white-gaitered red-legged soldier. He watched little brisk figures, figures whose movement was as the tick of the great Paris clock, take their smooth diagonal from point to point; the air had a taste as of something mixed with art, something that presented nature as a white-capped master-chef.

THE AMBASSADORS, Book 2, Chapter 2

Versailles, 1875

But all deserted palaces and gardens should be seen in the chill and leafless season. Then nature seems to give them up to your sympathy and they appear to take you into their confidence. The long, misty alleys and vistas were covered with a sort of brown and violet bloom which a painter would have loved to reproduce, but which a poor proser can only think of and sigh. As it melts away in the fringe of the gray treetops, or deepens in the recesses of the narrowing avenues, it is the most charming thing in the world. All the old Hebes and Floras and Neptunes were exposing their sallow nudities as if in compliment to the clemency of the weather. There is nowhere else, surely, such a redundancy of more or less chiseled marble; it is a forest of statues, as well as of trees.

PARISIAN SKETCHES

The Bellegardes' Château in Poitou

The *petit bourg* lay at the base of a huge mound, on the summit of which stood the crumbling ruins of a feudal castle, much of whose sturdy material, as well as that of the wall that dropped along the hill to enclose the clustered houses defensively, had been absorbed into the very substance of the village. The church was simply the former chapel of the castle, fronting upon its grass-grown court, which, however, was of generous enough width to have given up its quaintest corner to a small place of interment. Here the very headstones themselves seemed to sleep as they slanted into the grass; the patient elbow of the rampart held them together on one side, and in front, far beneath their mossy lids, the green plains and blue distances stretched away. The approach to the church, up the hill, defied all wheels. It was lined with peasants two or three rows deep, who stood watching old Madame de Bellegarde slowly ascend on the arm of her elder son and behind the pall-bearers of the other.

THE AMERICAN, Chapter 20

The Pont du Gard

I discovered in it a certain stupidity, a vague brutality. That element is rarely absent from great Roman work, which is wanting in the nice adaptation of the means to the end. The means are always exaggerated; the end is so much more than attained. The Roman rigor was apt to overshoot the mark, and I suppose a race which could do nothing small is as defective as a race that can do nothing great. Of this Roman rigor the Pont du Gard is an admirable example. It would be a great injustice, however, not to insist upon its beauty—a kind of manly beauty, that of an object constructed not to please but to serve, and impressive simply from the scale on which it carries out this intention. The preservation of the thing is extraordinary; nothing has crumbled or collapsed; every feature remains, and the huge blocks of stone, of a brownish-yellow, pile themselves, without mortar or cement, as evenly as the day they were laid together. All this to carry the water of a couple of springs to a little provincial city!

            A LITTLE TOUR IN FRANCE, Chapter 26

Scenes of Tension

The Narrator Meets the Egeria of the Long-Dead Poet Jeffrey Aspern

When I went back on the morrow the little maidservant conducted me straight through the long sala—it opened there as before in large perspective and was lighter now, which I thought a good omen—into a spacious shabby parlour with a fine old painted ceiling under which a strange figure sat alone at one of the windows. They come back to me now almost with the palpitation they caused, the successive states marking my consciousness that as the door of the room closed behind me I was really face to face with the Juliana of some of Aspern's most exquisite and most renowned lyrics. Then came a check from the perception that we weren't really face to face, inasmuch as she had over her eyes a horrible green shade which served for her almost as a mask. I believed for the instant that she had put it on expressly, so that from underneath it she might take me all in without my getting at herself. At the same time it created a presumption of some ghastly death's-head lurking behind it. The divine Juliana as a grinning skull—the vision hung there until it passed. Then it came to me that she *was* tremendously old—so old that death might take her at any moment, before I should have time to compass my end.

THE ASPERN PAPERS, Chapter 2

Isabel's First Doubt about Madame Merle

She considered, with the presumption of youth, that a morality differing from her own must be inferior to it; and this conviction was an aid to detecting an occasional flash of cruelty, an occasional lapse from candour, in the conversation of a person who had raised delicate kindness to an art and whose pride was too high for the narrow ways of deception. Her conception of human motives might, in certain lights, have been acquired at the court of some kingdom in decadence, and there were several in her list of which our heroine had not even heard.

THE PORTRAIT OF A LADY, Chapter 31

The Governess Encounters the Ghost of Peter Quint

I can say now neither what determined nor what guided me, but I went straight along the lobby, holding my candle high, till I came within sight of the tall window that presided over the great turn of the staircase. At this point I precipitately found myself aware of three things. They were practically simultaneous, yet they had flashes of succession. My candle, under a bold flourish, went out, and I perceived, by the uncovered window, that the yielding dusk of earliest morning rendered it unnecessary. Without it, the next instant, I knew that there was a figure on the stair. I speak of sequences, but I required no lapse of seconds to stiffen myself for a third encounter with Quint. The apparition had reached the landing halfway up and was therefore on the spot nearest the window, where, at sight of me, it stopped short and fixed me exactly as it had fixed me from the tower and from the garden. He knew me as well as I knew him; and so, in the cold faint twilight, with a glimmer in the high glass and another on the polish of the oak stair below, we faced each other in our common intensity.

THE TURN OF THE SCREW, Chapter 9

Millie Theale and Kate Croy

Certain aspects of the connection of these young women show for us, such is the twilight that gathers about them, in the likeness of some dim scene in a Maeterlinck play; we have positively the image, in the delicate dusk, of the figures so associated and yet so opposed, so mutually watchful: that of the angular, pale princess, ostrich-plumed, black robed, hung about with amulets, reminders, relics, mainly seated, mainly still, and that of the upright, restless, slow-circling lady of her court, who exchanges with her, across the black water streaked with evening gleams, fitful questions and answers.

THE WINGS OF THE DOVE, Chapter 24

The Man to Whom Nothing Is to Happen Discovers It

The escape would have been to love her; then, *then* he would have lived. *She* had lived—who could say now with what passion?—since she had loved him for himself; whereas he had never thought of her (ah how it hugely glared at him!) but in the chill of his egotism and the light of her use. Her spoken words came back to him—the chain stretched and stretched. The Beast had lurked indeed, and the Beast, at its hour, had sprung; it had sprung in that twilight of the cold April when, pale, ill, wasted, but all beautiful, and perhaps even then recoverable, she had risen from her chair to stand before him and let him imaginably guess. It had sprung as he didn't guess; it had sprung as she hopelessly turned from him, and the mark, by the time he left her, had fallen where it *was* to fall. He had justified his feat and achieved his fate; he had failed, with the last exactitude, of all he was to fail of; and a moan now rose to his lips as he remembered she had prayed he mightn't know.

THE BEAST IN THE JUNGLE

The Death of Daisy

A week after this the poor girl died; it had been indeed a terrible case of the *perniciosa*. A grave was found for her in the little Protestant cemetery, by an angle of the wall of imperial Rome, beneath the cypresses and the thick spring-flowers. Winterbourne stood there beside it with a number of other mourners; a number larger than the scandal excited by the young lady's career might have made probable. Near him stood Giovanelli, who came nearer still before Winterbourne turned away. Giovanelli, in decorous mourning, showed but a whiter face; his button-hole lacked its nosegay and he had visibly something urgent—and even to distress—to say, which he scarce knew how to "place." He decided at last to confide it with a pale convulsion to Winterbourne. "She was the most beautiful young lady I ever saw, and the most amiable." To which he added in a moment: "Also—naturally!—the most innocent."

DAISY MILLER, Chapter 4

Maggie's Eschewal of Hate

She continued to walk and continued to pause; she stopped afresh for the look into the smoking-room, and by this time—it was as if the recognition had of itself arrested her—she saw as in a picture, with the temptation she had fled from quite extinct, why it was she had been able to give herself from the first so little to the vulgar heat of her wrong. She might fairly, as she watched them, have missed it as a lost thing; have yearned for it, for the straight vindictive view, the rights of resentment, the rages of jealousy, the protests of passion, as for something she had been cheated of not least: a range of feelings which for many women would have meant so much, but which for *her* husband's wife, for her father's daughter, figured nothing nearer to experience than a wild eastern caravan, looming into view with crude colours in the sun, fierce pipes in the air, high spears against the sky, all a thrill, a natural joy to mingle with, but turning off short before it reached her and plunging into other defiles.

THE GOLDEN BOWL, Chapter 36

Maggie's Impulse to Spare Her Husband the Knowledge of What She Knows

There was even a minute, when her back was turned to him, during which she knew once more the strangeness of her desire to spare him, a strangeness that had already fifty times brushed her, in the depth of her trouble, as with the wild wing of some bird of the air who might blindly have swooped for an instant into the shaft of a well, darkening there by his momentary flutter the far-off round of sky. It was extraordinary, this quality in the taste of her wrong which made her completed sense of it seem rather to soften than to harden.

THE GOLDEN BOWL, Chapter 34

Strether Exhorts "Little" Bilham to "Live"

"It's not too late for *you*, on any side, and you don't strike me as in danger of missing the train; besides which people can be in general pretty well trusted, of course—with the clock of their freedom ticking as loud as it seems to do here—to keep an eye on the fleeting hour. All the same don't forget that you're young—blessedly young; be glad of it on the contrary and live up to it. Live all you can; it's a mistake not to. It doesn't so much matter what you do in particular, so long as you have your life. If you haven't had that what *have* you had? I see it now. I haven't done so enough before—and now I'm old; too old at any rate for what I see. The right time is any time that one is still so lucky as to have. You've plenty; that's the great thing; you're, as I say, damn you, so happily and hatefully young. Don't at any rate miss things out of stupidity. Of course I don't take you for a fool, or I shouldn't be addressing you thus awfully. Do what you like so long as you don't make *my* mistake. For it was a mistake. Live!"

THE AMBASSADORS, Book 5, Chapter 2

James's Notes for the Preceding

I was struck last evening with something that Jonathan Sturges, who has been staying here [Paris] 10 days, mentioned to me: it was only 10 words, but I seemed, as usual, to catch a glimpse of a *sujet de nouvelle* in it. We were talking of William Dean Howells and of his having seen him during a short and interrupted stay. Sturges said he seemed sad—rather brooding; and I asked him what gave him (Sturges) that impression. 'Oh—somewhere—I forget, when I was with him—he laid his hand on my shoulder and said *à propos* of some remark of mine: "Oh, you are young, you are young—be glad of it: be glad of it and *live*. Live all you can: it's a mistake not to. It doesn't so much matter what you do—but live. This place makes it all come over me. I see it now. I haven't done so—and now I'm old. It's too late. It has gone past me—I've lost it. You have time. You are young. Live!"' I amplify and improve a little—but that was the tone. It touches me—I can see him—I can hear him. Immediately, of course—as everything, thank God, does—it suggests a little situation.

THE NOTEBOOKS, October 31, 1895

Jackson Lemon Faces His Doom

Drop by drop the conviction had entered his mind that if his wife should return to England she would never again cross the Atlantic to the West. What she would do, how she would resist—this he was not yet prepared to tell himself; but he felt, every time he looked at her, that this beautiful woman whom he had adored was filled with a dumb, insuperable, ineradicable purpose. He knew that if she should plant herself, no power on earth would move her; and her blooming, antique beauty, and the general loftiness of her breeding, came to seem to him—rapidly—but the magnificent expression of a dense, patient, imperturbable obstinacy.

LADY BARBARINA, Chapter 6

Isabel's Disillusionment

Then the shadows had begun to gather; it was as if Osmond deliberately, almost malignantly, had put the lights out one by one. The dusk at first was vague and thin, and she could still see her way in it. But it steadily deepened, and if now and again it had occasionally lifted there were certain corners of her prospect that were impenetrably black. These shadows were not an emanation from her own mind: she was very sure of that; she had done her best to be just and temperate, to see only the truth. They were a part, they were a kind of creation and consequence, of her husband's very presence. They were not his misdeeds, his turpitudes; she accused him of nothing—that is but of one thing, which was *not* a crime. She knew of no wrong he had done; he was not violent, he was not cruel: she simply believed he hated her.

THE PORTRAIT OF A LADY, Chapter 42

Newman Imagines That He Hears Madame de Cintré's Voice

Suddenly there arose from the depths of the chapel, from behind the inexorable grating, a sound that drew his attention from the altar—the sound of a strange, lugubrious chant uttered by women's voices. It began softly, but it presently grew louder, and as it increased it became more of a wail and a dirge. It was the chant of the Carmelite nuns, their only human utterance. It was their dirge over their buried affections and over the vanity of earthly desires. At first he was bewildered, almost stunned, by the monstrous manifestation; then, as he comprehended its meaning, he listened intently and his heart began to throb. He listened for Madame de Cintré's voice, and in the very heart of the tuneless harmony he imagined he made it out.

THE AMERICAN, Chapter 24

"Venus Toute Entière a Sa Proie Attachée!"

I saw as I had never seen before what consuming passion can make of the marked mortal on whom, with fixed beak and claws, it has settled as on a prey. She reminded me of a sponge wrung dry and with fine pores agape. Voided and scraped of everything, her shell was merely crushable. So it was brought home to me that the victim could be abased, and so it disengaged itself from these things that the abasement could be conscious. I saw how it was that whereas, in such cases in general, people might have given up much, the sort of person this poor lady was could only give up everything. She was the absolute wreck of her storm, accordingly, but to which the pale ghost of a special sensibility still clung, waving from the mast, with a bravery that went to the heart, the last tatter of its flag.

THE SACRED FOUNT, Chapter 8

Miss Birdseye's Death

Miss Birdseye's voice was very low, like that of a person breathing with difficulty; but it had no painful nor querulous note—it expressed only the cheerful weariness which had marked all this last period of her life, and which seemed to make it now as blissful as it was suitable that she should pass away. Her head was thrown back against the top of the chair, the ribbon which confined her ancient hat hung loose, and the late afternoon-light covered her octogenarian face and gave it a kind of fairness, a double placidity. There was, to Ransom, something almost august in the trustful renunciation of her countenance; something in it seemed to say that she had been ready long before, but as the time was not ripe she had waited, with her usual faith that all was for the best; only, at present, since the right conditions met, she couldn't help feeling that it was quite a luxury, the greatest she had ever tasted. Miss Birdseye had given herself so lavishly all her life that it was rather odd there was anything left of her for the supreme surrender.

THE BOSTONIANS, Chapter 38

Writers and Other Artists

The Best-Seller (1)

I met her at some dinner and took her down, rather flattered at offering my arm to a celebrity. She didn't look like one, with her matronly mild inanimate face, but I supposed her greatness would come out in her conversation. I gave it all the opportunities I could, but was nevertheless not disappointed when I found her only a dull kind woman. This was why I liked her—she rested me so from literature. To myself literature was an irritation, a torment; but Greville Fane slumbered in the intellectual part of it even as a cat on a hearthrug or a Creole in a hammock. She could invent stories by the yard, but couldn't write a page of English. She went down to her grave without suspecting that though she had contributed volumes to the diversion of her contemporaries she hadn't contributed a sentence to the language.

GREVILLE FANE

Ouida

Frankly she was not sympathetic—and I scarce envy you the task of undertaking a book about her. But she was *curious*, in a common little way: she suggested somehow having come out of such a very "low-down" or even base little past, of unfathomable things, and yet being withal of a most uppish, or dauntless, little spirit of arrogance and independence. The best and most sincere thing about her I seemed to make out, was—or had been—her original genuine perception of the beauty, the distinction and quality of Italy: this almost inspired her—yet was mixed with such vulgarities and falsities too. She must have gone—and for many years—through absolute horror of growing poverty and final want—though for long too she was arrogant about her debts and obligations. The only way to treat her would be really, and quite frankly, I think, as a little terrible and finally pathetic *grotesque*; but even as such she *means* nothing—is too without form and void!

Letter to Elizabeth Lee, 1913

The Best-Seller (2)

It wasn't that when she tried to be what she called subtle, her fond consumers, bless them, didn't suspect the trick nor show what they thought of it: they straightway rose on the contrary to the morsel she had hoped to hold too high, and, making but a big cheerful bite of it, wagged their great collective tail artlessly for more. It was not given to her not to please, not granted even to her best refinements to affright.

THE NEXT TIME

Walter Pater

I think he has had—will have had—the most exquisite literary fortune: i.e. to have taken it out all, wholly, exclusively, with the pen (the style, the genius,) and absolutely not at all with the person. He is the mask without the face, and there isn't in his total superficies a tiny point of vantage for the newspaper to flap his wings on. You have been lively about him—but about whom *wouldn't* you be lively? I think you'd be lively about *me*!—Well, faint, pale, embarrassed, exquisite Pater! He reminds me, in the disturbed midnight of our actual literature, of one of those lucent matchboxes which you place, on going to bed, near the candle, to show you, in the darkness, where you can strike a light: he shines in the uneasy gloom—vaguely, and has a phosphorescence, not a flame. But I quite agree with you that he is not of the little day—but of the longer time.

Letter to Edmund Gosse, 1894

The Non-Seller

Several persons admired his books—nothing was less contestable; but they appeared to have a mortal objection to acquiring them by subscription or by purchase: they begged or borrowed or stole, they delegated one of the party perhaps to commit the volumes to memory and repeat them, like the bards of old, to listening multitudes. Some ingenious theory was required at any rate to account for the inexorable limits of his circulation.

THE NEXT TIME

Belated Success

The big blundering newspaper had discovered him, and now he was proclaimed and anointed and crowned. His place was assigned him as publicly as if a fat usher with a wand had pointed to the topmost chair; he was to pass up and still up, higher and higher, between the watching faces and the envious sounds—away up to the dais and the throne. In a flash, somehow, all was different; the tremendous wave I speak of had swept something away. It had knocked down, I suppose, my little customary altar, my twinkling tapers and my flowers, and had reared itself into the likeness of a temple vast and bare. When Neil Paraday should come out of the house he would come out a contemporary. That was what had happened: the poor man was to be squeezed into his horrible age.

THE DEATH OF A LION

The Old Artist

"There are two moods," I remember his saying, "in which we may walk through galleries—the critical and the ideal. They seize us at their pleasure, and we can never tell which is to take its turn. The critical, oddly, is the genial one, the friendly, the condescending. It relishes the pretty trivialities of art, its vulgar cleverness, its conscious graces. It has a kindly greeting for anything which looks as if, according to his light, the painter had enjoyed doing it—for the little Dutch cabbages and kettles, for the taper fingers and breezy mantles of late-coming Madonnas, for the little blue-hilled, broken-bridged, pastoral, classical landscapes. Then there are the days of fierce, fastidious longing—solemn church-feasts of the taste or the faith—when all vulgar effort and all petty success is a weariness and everything but the best, the best of the best, disgusts. In these hours we're relentless aristocrats of attitude. We'll not take Michael for granted, we'll not swallow Raphael whole!"

THE MADONNA OF THE FUTURE

The Actress

"I was looking for you; he had prepared me. We are such old friends!" said the actress, in a tone courteously exempt from intention: upon which Sherringham again took her hand and raised it to his lips, with a tenderness which her whole appearance seemed to bespeak for her, a sort of practical consideration and carefulness of touch, as if she were an object precious and frail, an instrument for producing rare sounds, to be handled, like a legendary violin, with a recognition of its value.

THE TRAGIC MUSE, Chapter 21

Lord Northmore's Letters

She faced it, after dinner, in her little closed drawing-room, unwrapping the two volumes—*The Public and Private Correspondence of the Right Honourable*, etc., etc.,—and looking well, first, at the great escutcheon on the purple cover and at the various portraits within, so numerous that wherever she opened she came on one. It had not been present to her before that he was so perpetually "sitting," but he figured in every phase and in every style, and the gallery was enriched with views of his successive residences, each one a little grander than the last.

THE ABASEMENT OF THE NORTHMORES

Society and Art

If he and she together, and her great field and future (the stage), and the whole cause they had armed and declared for, have not been serious things they have been base make-believes and trivialities—which is what in fact the homage of society to art always turns out so soon as art presumes not to be vulgar and futile. It is immensely the fashion and immensely edifying to listen to, this homage, while it confines its attention to vanities and frauds; but it knows only terror, feels only horror, the moment that, instead of making all the concessions, art proceeds to ask for a few.

Preface to THE TRAGIC MUSE

New York

The Harbor

The aspect the power wears then is indescribable; it is the power of the most extravagant of cities, rejoicing, as with the voice of the morning, in its might, its fortune, its unsurpassable conditions, and imparting to every object and element, to the motion and expression of every floating, hurrying, panting thing, to the throb of ferries and tugs, to the plash of waves and the play of winds and the glint of lights and the shrill of whistles and the quality and authority of breeze-borne cries—all, practically, a diffused, wasted clamour of *detonations*—something of its sharp free accent and, above all, of its sovereign sense of being "backed" and able to back.

THE AMERICAN SCENE, Chapter 2

The Waldorf-Astoria Lobby

The hundreds and hundreds of people in circulation, the innumerable huge-hatted ladies in especial, with their air of finding in the gilded and storied labyrinth the very firesides and pathways of home, became thus the serene faithful, whose rites one would no more have sceptically brushed than one would doff one's disguise in a Mohammedan mosque. The question of who they all might be, seated under palms and by fountains, or communing, to some inimitable New York tune, with the shade of Marie Antoinette in the queer recaptured actuality of an easy Versailles or an intimate Trianon—such questions as that, interesting in other societies and at other times, insisted on yielding here to the mere eloquence of the general truth. Here was a social order in positively stable equilibrium. Here was a world whose relation to its form and medium was practically imperturbable; here was a conception of publicity *as* the vital medium organized with the authority with which the American genius for organization, put on its mettle, alone could organize it.

THE AMERICAN SCENE, Chapter 2

Central Park

That is how we see Central Park, utterly overdone by the "run" on its resources, yet also never having had to make an excuse. When once we have taken in thus its remarkable little history, there is no endearment of appreciation that we are not ready to lay, as a tribute, on its breast; with the interesting effect, besides, of our recognizing in this light how the place has had to be, in detail and feature, exactly what it is. It has had to have something for everybody, since everybody arrives famished; it has had to multiply itself to extravagance, to pathetic little efforts of exaggeration and deception, to be, breathlessly, everywhere and everything at once, and produce on the spot the particular romantic object demanded, lake or river or cataract, wild woodland or teeming garden, boundless vista or bosky nook, noble eminence or smiling valley. It has had to have feature at any price.

THE AMERICAN SCENE, Chapter 4

The Day School

I remember infuriated ushers, of foreign speech and flushed complexion—the tearing across of hapless "exercises" and *dictées* and the hurtle through the air of dodged volumes; only never, despite this, the extremity of smiting. There can have been at the Institution no blows instructionally dealt—nor even from our hours of ease do any such echoes come back to me. Little Cubans and Mexicans, I make out, were not to be vulgarly whacked—in deference, presumably, to some latent relic or imputed survival of Castilian pride; which would impose withal considerations of quite practical prudence.

A SMALL BOY AND OTHERS, Chapter 15

Millie Theale

It was New York mourning, it was New York hair, it was a New York history, confused as yet, but multitudinous, of the loss of parents, brothers, sisters, almost every human appendage, all on a scale and with a sweep that had required the greater stage; it was a New York legend of affecting, of romantic isolation, and, beyond everything, it was by most accounts, in respect to the mass of money so piled on the girl's back, a set of New York possibilities. She was alone, she was stricken, she was rich, and, in particular, she was strange—a combination in itself of a nature to engage Mrs. Stringham's attention.

THE WINGS OF THE DOVE, Chapter 5

The Elevator

The sempiternal lift, for one's comings and goings, affects one at last as an almost intolerable symbol of the herded and driven state and of that malady of preference for gregarious ways, of insistence on gregarious ways only, by which the people about one seem ridden. To wait, perpetually, in a human bunch, in order to be hustled, under military drill, the imperative order to "step lively," into some tight mechanic receptacle, fearfully and wonderfully working, is conceivable, no doubt, as a sad liability of our nature, but represents surely, when cherished and sacrificed to, a strange perversion of sympathies and ideals.

THE AMERICAN SCENE, Chapter 4

The Lonely Author in a City of Commerce

Such an unfortunate, even at the time I speak of, had still to confess to the memory of a not inconsiderably earlier season when, seated for several months at the very moderate altitude of Twenty-Fifth Street, he felt himself day by day alone in that scale of the balance; alone, I mean, with the music-masters and French pastry-cooks, the ladies and children—immensely present and immensely numerous these, but testifying with a collective voice to the extraordinary absence (save as pieced together through a thousand gaps and indirectnesses) of a serious male interest. The question was to remain, this interrogated mystery of what American town-life had left to entertain the observer withal when nineteen twentieths of it, or in other words the huge organised mystery of the consummately, the supremely applied money-passion, were inexorably closed to him.

Preface to DAISY MILLER

Manhattan Winter

She saw that it was great fun to be a woman in America, and that this was the best way to enjoy the New York winter—the wonderful, brilliant New York winter, the queer, long-shaped, glittering city, the heterogeneous hours, among which you couldn't tell the morning from the afternoon or the night from either of them, the perpetual liberties and walks, the rushings-out and the droppings-in, the intimacies, the endearments, the comicalities, the sleigh-bells, the cutters, the sunsets on the snow, the ice-parties in the frosty clearness, the bright, hot, velvety houses, the bouquets, the bonbons, the little cakes, the big cakes, the irrepressible inspirations of shopping, the innumerable luncheons and dinners that were offered to youth and innocence, the quantities of chatter of quantities of girls, the perpetual motion of the German, the suppers at restaurants after the play, the way in which life was pervaded by Delmonico.

LADY BARBARINA, Chapter 5

Julia's Last Beau

Yes, it described him to say that, in addition to all the rest of him, and of *his* personal history, and of his family, and of theirs, in addition to their social posture, as that of a serried phalanx, and to their notoriously enormous wealth and crushing respectability, she might have been ever so much less lovely for him if she had been only— well, a little prepared to answer questions. And it was n't as if, quiet, cultivated, earnest, public-spirited, brought up in Germany, infinitely travelled, awfully like a high-caste Englishman, and all the other pleasant things, it was n't as if he did n't love to be with her, to look at her, just as she was; for he loved it exactly as much, so far as that footing simply went, as any free and foolish youth who had ever made the last demonstration of it. It was that marriage was for him—and for them all, the serried Frenches—a great matter, a goal to which a man of intelligence, a real shy beautiful man of the world, did n't hop on one foot, did n't skip and jump, as if he were playing an urchins' game, but toward which he proceeded with a deep and anxious, a noble and highly just deliberation.

JULIA BRIDE, Chapter 1

Literary Criticism

The Seasons in Fiction

Why is it that the life that overflows in Dickens seems to me always to go on in the morning, or in the very earliest hours of the afternoon at most, and in a vast apartment that appears to have windows, large, uncurtained, and rather unwashed windows, on all sides at once? Why is it that in George Eliot the sun sinks forever to the west, and the shadows are long, and the afternoon wanes, and the trees vaguely rustle, and the color of the day is much inclined to yellow? Why is it that in Charlotte Brontë we move through an endless autumn? Why is it that in Jane Austen we sit quite resigned in an arrested spring? Why does Hawthorne give us the afternoon hour later than any one else?—oh, late, late, quite uncannily late, and as if it were always winter outside?

THE LESSON OF BALZAC

Balzac

He collected his experience within himself; no other economy explains his achievement; this thrift alone, remarkable yet thinkable, embodies the necessary miracle. His system of cellular confinement, in the interest of the miracle, was positively that of a Benedictine monk, leading his life within the four walls of his convent and bent, the year round, over the smooth parchment on which, with wondrous illumination and enhancement of gold and crimson and blue, he inscribed the glories of the faith and the legends of the saints.

THE LESSON OF BALZAC

Swinburne's Prose Style

But with this extravagant development of the imagination there is no commensurate development either of the reason or of the moral sense. One of these defects is, to our mind, fatal to Mr. Swinburne's style; the other is fatal to his tone, to his temper, to his critical pretensions. His style is without measure, without discretion, without sense of what to take and what to leave; after a few pages, it becomes intolerably fatiguing. It is always listening to itself—always turning its head over its shoulders to see its train flowing behind it. The train shimmers and tumbles in a very gorgeous fashion, but the rustle of its embroidery is fatally importunate.

VIEWS AND REVIEWS

Emma Bovary and Frédéric Moreau

Why did Flaubert choose, as special conduits of the life he proposed to depict, such inferior and in the case of Frédéric such abject human specimens? I insist only in respect to the latter, the perfection of *Madame Bovary* scarce leaving one much warrant for wishing anything other. Even here, however, the general scale and size of Emma, who is small even of her sort, should be a warning to hyperbole. If I say that in the matter of Frédéric at all events the answer is inevitably detrimental I mean that it weighs heavily on our author's general credit. He wished in each case to make a picture of experience—middling experience, it is true—and of the world close to him, but if he imagined nothing better for his purpose than such a heroine and such a hero, both such limited reflectors and registers, we are forced to believe it to have been by a defect of his mind.

NOTES ON NOVELISTS

Zola (1)

Once upon a time a rather pretentious person, whose moral tone had been corrupted by evil communications, and who lived among a set of people equally pretentious, but regrettably low-minded, being in conversation with another person, a lady of great robustness of judgement and directness of utterance, made use constantly, in a somewhat cynical and pessimistic sense, of the expression, "the world—the world." At last the distinguished listener could bear it no longer, and abruptly made reply: "My poor lady, do you call that corner of a pigsty in which you happen to live, *the world?*" Some such answer as this we are moved to make to M. Zola's naturalism. Does he call that vision of things of which *Nana* is a representation, *nature?* The mighty mother, in her blooming richness, seems to blush from brow to chin at the insult! On what authority does M. Zola represent nature to us as a combination of the cesspool and the house of prostitution? On what authority does he represent foulness rather than fairness as the sign that we are to know her by? On the authority of his predilections alone, and this is his great trouble and the weak point of his incontestably remarkable talent.

Review of NANA

James Speculates That His Play-Writing Years May Not Have Been Wasted

Has a *part* of all this wasted passion and squandered time been simply the precious lesson, taught me in that roundabout and devious, that cruelly expensive, way, *of the singular value for a narrative plan too* of the divine principle of the Scenario? If that *has* been one side of the moral of the whole unspeakable, the whole tragic experience, I almost bless the pangs and the pains and the miseries of it. IF there has lurked in the central core of it this exquisite truth—I almost hold my breath with suspense as I try to formulate it; so much, *so much*, hangs radiantly there as depending on it—this exquisite truth that what I call the divine principle in question is a key that, working in the same *general* way fits the complicated chambers of *both* the dramatic and the narrative lock: IF, I say, I have crept round through long apparent barrenness, through suffering and sadness intolerable, to that rare perception—why my infinite little loss is converted into an almost infinite little gain.

THE NOTEBOOKS, February 14, 1895

Zola (2)

He describes what he best feels, and feels it more and more as it naturally comes to him—quite, if I may allow myself the image, as we zoologically see some mighty animal, a beast of a corrugated hide and a portentous snout, soaking with joy in the warm ooze of an African riverside.

NOTES ON NOVELISTS

Henry James to His French Translator, Who Gave Up on *A Small Boy and Others*

Translation is an effort—though a most flattering one!—to *tear* the hapless flesh, and in fact to get rid of so much of it that the living thing bleeds and faints away! forgive the violence of my figure. I believe truly that I feel myself to have lost less blood at your hands than (in those past little adventures) I could have done at any other's. But without having in the least sought the effect, it does interest me, it does even partly exhilarate me to recognize that the small Boy, while yet so tame and intrinsically safe a little animal, is locked fast in the golden cage of the *intraduisible*! It's all the more genial of you to look at him so patiently through that gilt wire of the bars.

Letter to Auguste Monod, 1913

Zola (3)

"The matter with" Zola then, so far as it goes, was that, as the imagination of the artist is in the best cases not only clarified but intensified by his equal possession of Taste (deserving here if ever the old-fashioned honor of a capital), so when he has lucklessly never inherited that auxiliary blessing the imagination itself inevitably breaks down as a consequence. There is simply no limit, in fine, to the misfortune of being tasteless; it does not merely disfigure the surface and the fringe of your performance—it eats back into the very heart and enfeebles the sources of life. When you have no taste you have no discretion, which is the conscience of taste, and when you have no discretion you perpetrate books like *Rome*, which are without intellectual modesty, books like *Fécondité*, which are without a sense of the ridiculous, books like *Vérité*, which are without the finer vision of human experience.

NOTES ON NOVELISTS

The Russian Novelists

Don't let anyone persuade you—there are plenty of ignorant and fatuous duffers to try to do it—that strenuous selection and comparison are not the very essence of art, and that Form *is* [not] substance to that degree that there is absolutely no substance without it. Form alone *takes*, and holds and preserves, substance—saves it from the welter of helpless verbiage that we swim in as in a sea of tasteless tepid pudding, and that makes one ashamed of an art capable of such degradations. Tolstoi and D. [Dostoievski] are fluid pudding, though not tasteless, because the amount of their own minds and souls in solution in the broth gives it savour and flavour, thanks to the strong, rank quality of their genius and their experience. But there are all sorts of things to be said of them, and in particular that we see how great a vice is their lack of composition, their defiance of economy and architecture, directly they are emulated and imitated; *then*, as subjects of emulation, models, they quite give themselves away.

Letter to Hugh Walpole, 1912

The Brontës

The romantic tradition of the Brontës, with posterity, has been still more essentially helped, I think, by a force independent of any one of their applied faculties—by the attendant image of their dreary, their tragic history, their loneliness and poverty of life. That picture has been made to hang before us as insistently as the vividest page of *Jane Eyre* or of *Wuthering Heights*. If these things were "stories," as we say, and stories of a lively interest, the medium from which they sprang was above all in itself a story, such a story as has fairly elbowed out the rights of appreciation, as has come at last to impose itself as an expression of the power concerned. The personal position of the three sisters, of the two in particular, had been marked, in short, with so sharp an accent that this accent has become for us the very tone of their united production.

THE LESSON OF BALZAC

The Art of The Novel

The Artist as a Privileged Person

Here lurks an immense homage to the general privilege of the artist, to that constructive, that creative passion—portentous words, but they are convenient—the exercise of which finds so many an occasion for appearing to him the highest of human fortunes, the rarest boon of the gods. He values it, all sublimely and perhaps a little fatuously, for itself—as the great extension, great beyond all others, of experience and of consciousness; with the toil and trouble a mere sun-cast shadow that falls, shifts and vanishes, the result of his living in so large a light. On the constant nameless felicity of this Robert Louis Stevenson has, in an admirable passage (and as in so many other connexions), said the right word: that the partaker of the "life of art" who repines at the absence of the rewards, as they are called, of the pursuit might surely be better occupied.

Preface to THE AMERICAN

The Art of the Romancer

The balloon of experience is in fact of course tied to the earth, and under that necessity we swing, thanks to a rope of remarkable length, in the more or less commodious car of the imagination; but it is by the rope we know where we are, and from the moment that cable is cut we are at large and unrelated: we only swing apart from the globe—though remaining as exhilarated, naturally, as we like, especially when all goes well. The art of the romancer is, "for the fun of it," insidiously to cut the cable, to cut it without our detecting him.

Preface to THE AMERICAN

The Site of Composition

I had rooms on Riva Schiavoni, at the top of a house near the passage leading off to San Zaccaria; the waterside life, the wondrous lagoon spread before me, and the ceaseless human chatter of Venice came in at my windows, to which I seem to myself to have been constantly driven, in the fruitless fidget of composition, as if to see whether, out in the blue channel, the ship of some right suggestion, of some better phrase, of the next happy twist of my subject, the next true touch for my canvas, might n't come into sight. But I recall vividly enough that the response most elicited, in general, to these restless appeals was the rather grim admonition that romantic and historic sites, such as the land of Italy abounds in, offer the artist a questionable aid to concentration when they themselves are not to be the subject of it.

Preface to THE PORTRAIT OF A LADY

London through Different Eyes

I arrived so at the history of little Hyacinth Robinson—he sprang up for me out of the London pavement. To find his possible adventure interesting I had only to conceive his watching the same public show, the same innumerable appearances, I had watched myself, and of his watching very much as I had watched; save indeed for one little difference. This difference would be that so far as all the swarming facts should speak of freedom and ease, knowledge and power, money, opportunity and satiety, he should be able to revolve round them but at the most respectful of distances and with every door of approach shut in his face. For one's self, all conveniently, there had been doors that opened—opened into light and warmth and cheer, into good and charming relations; and if the place as a whole lay heavy on one's consciousness there was yet always for relief this implication of one's own lucky share of the freedom and ease, lucky acquaintance with the number of lurking springs at light pressure of which particular vistas would begin to recede, great lighted, furnished, peopled galleries, sending forth gusts of agreeable sound.

       Preface to THE PRINCESS CASAMASSIMA

Here and There

The Germ of a Novel (1)

I might envy, though I couldn't emulate, the imaginative writer so constituted as to see his fable first and to make out its agents afterwards: I could think so little of any fable that didn't need its agents positively to launch it; I could think so little of any situation that didn't depend for its interest on the nature of the persons situated, and thereby on their way of taking it.

Preface to THE PORTRAIT OF A LADY

The Germ of a Novel (2)

So it was, at any rate, that when my amiable friend, on the Christmas Eve, before the table that glowed safe and fair through the brown London night, spoke of such an odd matter as that a good lady in the north, always well looked on, was at daggers drawn with her only son, ever hitherto exemplary, over the ownership of the valuable furniture of a fine old house just accruing to the young man by his father's death, I instantly became aware, with my "sense for the subject," of the prick of inoculation; the *whole* of the virus, as I have called it, being infused by that single touch.

Preface to THE SPOILS OF POYNTON

Remembrance of Things Past

I foresee moreover how little I shall be able to resist, throughout these Notes, the force of persuasion expressed in the individual *vivid* image of the past wherever encountered, these images having always such terms of their own, such subtle secrets and insidious arts for keeping us in relation with them, for bribing us by the beauty, the authority, the wonder of their saved intensity. They have saved it, they seem to say to us, from such a welter of death and darkness and ruin that this alone makes a value and a light and a dignity for them, something indeed of an argument that our story, since we attempt to tell one, has lapses and gaps without them.

THE MIDDLE YEARS, Chapter 1

Gabriel Nash's Credo

"And why should one call one's self anything? One only deprives other people of their dearest occupation. Let me add that you don't *begin* to have an insight into the art of life till it ceases to be of the smallest consequence to you what you may be called. That's rudimentary."

THE TRAGIC MUSE, Chapter 2

Mrs. Gereth's Idea of a Mother's Due

One's mother, gracious heaven, if one were the kind of fine young man one ought to be, the only kind Mrs. Gereth cared for, was a subject for poetry, for idolatry. Hadn't she often told Fleda of her friend Madame de Jaume, the wittiest of women, but a small, black crooked person, each of whose three boys, when absent, wrote to her every day of their lives? She had the house in Paris, she had the house in Poitou, she had more than in the lifetime of her husband (to whom, in spite of her appearance, she had afforded repeated cause for jealousy), because she had to the end of her days the supreme word about everything. It was easy to see that Mrs. Gereth would have given again and again her complexion, her figure, and even perhaps the spotless virtue she had still more successfully retained, to have been the consecrated Madame de Jaume.

THE SPOILS OF POYNTON, Chapter 5

Mrs. Newsome and Sarah Pocock

Mrs. Newsome was the only woman he had known, even at Woollett, as to whom his conviction was positive that to lie was beyond her art. Sarah Pocock, for instance, her own daughter, though with social ideals, as they said, in some respects different—Sarah who *was*, in her way, aesthetic, had never refused to human commerce that mitigation of rigour; there were occasions when he had distinctly seen her apply it.

THE AMBASSADORS, Book 2, Chapter 2

Strether's Lost Son

He had again and again made out for himself that he might have kept his little boy, his little dull boy who had died at school of rapid diphtheria, if he had not in those years so insanely given himself to merely missing the mother. It was the soreness of his remorse that the child had in all likelihood not really been dull—had been dull, as he had been banished and neglected, mainly because the father had been unwittingly selfish. This was doubtless but the secret habit of sorrow, which had slowly given way to time; yet there remained an ache sharp enough to make the spirit, at the sight now and again of some fair young man just growing up, wince with the thought of an opportunity lost.

THE AMBASSADORS, Book 2, Chapter 2

Breach of Promise

That she had pretended she loved him was comparatively nothing; other women had pretended it, and other women too had really done it; but that she had pretended he could possibly have been right and safe and blest in loving *her*, a creature of the kind who could sniff that squalor of the law-court, of claimed damages and brazen lies and published kisses, of love-letters read amid obscene guffaws, as a positive tonic to resentment, as a high incentive to her course—this was what put him so beautifully in the right.

THE BENCH OF DESOLATION

Dusk

There was a general shade in all the lower reaches—a fine clear dusk in garden and grove, a thin suffusion of twilight out of which the greater things, the high treetops and pinnacles, the long crests of motionless wood and chimnied roof, rose into golden air. The last calls of birds sounded extraordinarily loud; they were like the timed, serious splashes, in wide, still water, of divers not expecting to rise again.

THE SACRED FOUNT, Chapter 8

The Lady's Train

These ladies were apparently persons of high fashion, they were dressed with great splendour and their long silken trains and furbelows were spread over the polished floor. It was on their dresses the young woman had fixed her eyes, though what she was thinking of I am unable to say. I hazard the hypothesis of her mutely remarking that to carry about such a mass of ponderable pleasure would surely be one of the highest uses of freedom.

THE AMERICAN, Chapter 11

Lady Agnes

Lady Agnes did justice to the natural rule in virtue of which it usually comes to pass that a woman doesn't get on with her husband's female belongings, and was even willing to be sacrificed to it in her disciplined degree. But she desired not to be sacrificed for nothing: if she was to be objected to as a mother-in-law she wished to be the mother-in-law first.

THE TRAGIC MUSE, Chapter 5

Sentences and Phrases

... Mr. Verver whose easy way with his millions had taxed to such small purpose, in the arrangements, the principle of reciprocity.

THE GOLDEN BOWL, Chapter 1

So does a poor old croaking barnyard fowl advise a golden eagle!

Letter to Edith Wharton, 1909

I have simply lain stretched, a faithful old veteran slave, upon the doormat of your palace of adventure.

Letter to Edith Wharton, 1914

We stand like a race with shrunken muscles, staring helplessly at the weights our forefathers easily lifted.

RODERICK HUDSON, Chapter 6

Madame de Bellegarde resembled her daughter as an insect might resemble a flower.

THE AMERICAN, Chapter 10

... the grey town library of Blackport-on-Dwindle, all granite, fog and female fiction.

THE BIRTHPLACE

Lady Agnes wore the countenance she might have shown at the theatre in a place where pistols were fired.

THE TRAGIC MUSE, Chapter 8

... a visiting list which bulged and contracted in the wrong places, like a country made garment.

THE BOSTONIANS, Chapter 10

... the strange sound of her laugh, which was as if the faint "walking" ghost of her old-time tone had suddenly cut a caper.

THE ASPERN PAPERS, Chapter 6

... the moustachioed personage round whose name Mrs. Maule would probably have caused detrimental anecdote most thickly to cluster.

JULIA BRIDE, Chapter 2

She had been buried in a London suburb, a part then of Nature's breast, but which he had seen lose one after another every feature of freshness.

                    THE ALTAR OF THE DEAD

Her life was like a room prepared for a dance: the furniture was all against the walls.

                    THE OTHER HOUSE, Chapter 1

. . . made sociability a cool, public, out-of-door affair, without a secret or a mystery—confined it, as one might say, to the breezy, sunny forecourt of the temple of friendship, forbidding it any dream of access to the obscure and comparatively stuffy interior.

                    THE OTHER HOUSE, Chapter 19

Doctor Ramage was a little man who moved, with a warning air, on tiptoe, as if he were playing some drawing-room game of surprises, and who had a face so candid and circular that it suggested a large white pill.

                    THE OTHER HOUSE, Chapter 3

Greville Fane's French and Italian were droll; the imitative faculty had been denied her, and she had an unequalled gift, especially pen in hand, of squeezing big mistakes into small opportunities.

GREVILLE FANE

This was the weariness of every fresh meeting; he dealt out lies as he might the cards from the greasy old pack for the game of diplomacy to which you were to sit down with him.

THE WINGS OF THE DOVE, Chapter 1

"It's what they call a marriage of reason," she once had said; "that means, you know, a marriage of madness."

RODERICK HUDSON, Chapter 19

He instantly admitted his visitor, who came in with the air of the ambassador of a great power meeting the delegate of a barbarous tribe whom an absurd accident had enabled for the moment to be abominably annoying.

THE AMERICAN, Chapter 24

He knew the small vista of her street, closed at the end and as dreary as an empty pocket, where the pairs of shabby little houses, semi-detached but indissolubly united were like married couples on bad terms.

THE ALTAR OF THE DEAD

He wondered gloomily, at any rate, whether for men of his friend's large easy power there was not an ampler moral law than for narrow mediocrities like himself, who, yielding Nature a meagre interest on her investment (such as it was), had no reason to expect from her this affectionate laxity as to their accounts.

RODERICK HUDSON, Chapter 9

Mrs. Light told me in Florence that she had given her child the education of a princess. In other words I suppose she speaks three or four languages and has read several hundred French novels.

RODERICK HUDSON, Chapter 8

This edition is limited to 500 copies